STUDENT BOOK

GW00993635

WorldView
3B

MICHAEL ROST

Gillie Cunningham   **Sue Mohamed**
Robin Wileman   **Araminta Crace**   **Terra Brockman**

Simon Greenall
Series Editor, British English edition

Longman

WorldView Student Book 3B

Authorized adaptation from the United Kingdom edition entitled
Language to Go, First Edition, published by Pearson Education
Limited publishing under its Longman imprint.
Copyright © 2002 by Pearson Education Limited

All rights reserved.
No part of this publication may be reproduced,
stored in a retrieval system, or transmitted
in any form or by any means, electronic, mechanical,
photocopying, recording, or otherwise,
without the prior permission of the publisher.

American English adaptation published by Pearson Education,
Inc. Copyright © 2005.

Pearson Education, 10 Bank Street, White Plains, NY 10606

Editorial director: Pamela Fishman
Project manager: Irene Frankel
Senior acquisitions editor: Virginia L. Blanford
Senior development editors: Robin Longshaw, José Antonio Méndez
Vice president, director of design and production: Rhea Banker
Executive managing editor: Linda Moser
Associate managing editor: Mike Kemper
Production editor: Sasha Kintzler
Art director: Elizabeth Carlson
Vice president, director of international marketing: Bruno Paul
Senior manufacturing buyer: Edie Pullman
Text and cover design: Elizabeth Carlson
Photo research: Aerin Csigay
Text composition: Word and Image Design
Text font: 10.5/13pt Utopia and 10/12pt Frutiger Bold

ISBN: 0-13-184696-5

Library of Congress Control Number: 2003065959

Printed in the United States of America
1 2 3 4 5 6 7 8 9 10–BAM–09 08 07 06 05 04

Text Credits
Page 97, You've Got a Friend. Words and music by Carole King. ©
1971 (Renewed 1999) Colgems-EMI Music Inc. All rights reserved.
International copyright secured. Used by permission. 135, If I
Could Turn Back Time. Words and music by Diane Warren. ©1989
Realsongs (ASCAP). All rights reserved. Used by permission.

Illustration Credits
Steve Attoe, pp. 102, 106; Paul McCusker, 81; Stephen Quinlan, 96.

Photo Credits
Page 68, Trevor Clifford; 69, Trevor Clifford; 71, Erlanson
Productions/Getty Images; 72, *(left)* Howard Huang/Getty Images,
(left bottom) Getty Images, *(right)* Zefa Visual Media -
Germany/Index Stock Imagery, *(middle)* Michael Keller/Corbis,
(bottom right) Thomas Del Brase/Getty Images; 73, Corbis
Images/PictureQuest; 75, *(left)* Pictor International, *(middle)*
Powerstock Zefa/Benelux Press, *(right)* ActionPlus/Neale Haynes;
76, Professional Sport/ImageState-Pictor/PictureQuest; 77, *(left)*
Magnum/Peter Marlow, *(right)* Magnum/Peter Marlow; 78,
ThinkStock LLC/Index Stock Imagery; 82, *(top left)* Junko
Kimura/Getty Images, *(top right)* Terry McCormick/Getty Images,
(bottom) Steve Mason/Photodisc/ PictureQuest; 84, Adam
Smith/Getty Images; 86, *(background)* Powerstock Zefa, *(left)*
World Pictures, *(A-H)* Trevor Clifford; 88, Glen Allison/Getty
Images; 90, *(top right)* Columbia/Sony/The Kobal Collection,
(bottom right) Stephane Cardinale/Corbis, *(left)* Dreamworks
LLC/The Kobal Collection; 92, Digital Vision /Getty Images; 95,
Trevor Clifford; 96, Neal Preston/Corbis; 98, *(top right)*
Images.com/Corbis, *(bottom left)* Randy Faris/Corbis; 99, *(left)*
Stuart McClymont /Getty Images; 104, Bettmann/Corbis; 105,
Bettmann/Corbis; 107, Gareth Boden; 108, Corbis
Images/PictureQuest; 112, Stewart Cohen/Index Stock Imagery;
113, *(left)* Michael Keller/Corbis, *(right)* ITStock Int'l/eStock
Photo/PictureQuest; 117, Mark Hunt/Index Stock Imagery; 120,
(top) Corbis Stock Market/Peter Beek, *(bottom)* Corbis Stock
Market/Jon Feingersh; 121, *(right)* Telegraph Picture Library/M.
Krasowitz; 123, William Thomas Cain/Getty Images; 126, Digital
Vision/Getty Images; 128, Superstock; 130, Digital Vision/Getty
Images; 133, *(left)* Bill Bachmann/PhotoEdit, *(middle left)* Richard
Klune/Corbis, *(middle right)* Jonathan Nourok/PhotoEdit, *(right)*
Forest Johnson/Corbis; 135, Robert Mora/Getty Images.

Introduction

Welcome to *WorldView*, a four-level English course for adults and young adults. *WorldView* builds fluency by exploring a wide range of compelling topics presented from an international perspective. A trademark two-page lesson design, with clear and attainable language goals, ensures that students feel a sense of accomplishment and increased self-confidence in every class.

WorldView's approach to language learning follows a simple and proven **MAP**:
• **M**otivate learning through stimulating content and achievable learning goals.
• **A**nchor language production with strong, focused language presentations.
• **P**ersonalize learning through engaging and communicative speaking activities.

Course components

The *WorldView Student Book with Student Audio CD* and the *Workbook* are available in both full and split editions.

• **Student Book with Student Audio CD** *(Split Edition)*
The **Student Book** contains 14, four-page units; periodic Review Units; two World of Music Units; Information for Pair and Group Work; a Vocabulary list; and a Grammar Reference section.

The Student Audio CD includes tracks for all pronunciation and listening exercises (or reading texts, in selected units) in the *Student Book*. The *Student Audio CD* can be used with the *Student Book* for self-study and coordinates with the *Workbook* listening and pronunciation exercises.

• For each activity in the *Student Book*, the interleaved **Teacher's Edition** provides step-by-step procedures and exercise answer keys as well as a wealth of teacher support: unit Warm-ups, Optional Activities, Extensions, Culture Notes, Background Information, Teaching Tips, Wrap-ups, and extensive Language Notes. In addition, the *Teacher's Edition* includes a course orientation guide, full audio scripts, and the *Workbook* answer key.

• **The Workbook** *(Split Edition)* has 14 three-page units that correspond to each of the *Student Book* units. Used in conjunction with the *Student Audio CD*, the *Workbook* provides abundant review and practice activities for Vocabulary, Grammar, Listening, and Pronunciation, along with periodic Self-quizzes. A Learning Strategies section at the beginning of the *Workbook* helps students to be active learners.

• **The Class Audio Program** is available in either CD or cassette format and contains all the recorded material for in-class use.

• **The Teacher's Resource Book** (with **Testing Audio CD** and **TestGen Software**) has three sections of reproducible material: extra communication activities for in-class use, model writing passages for each *Student Book* writing assignment, and a complete testing program: seven quizzes and two tests, along with scoring guides and answer keys. Also included are an *Audio CD* for use with the quizzes and tests and an easy-to-use TestGen software CD for customizing the tests.

• For each level of the full course, the ***WorldView* Video** presents seven, five-minute authentic video segments connected to *Student Book* topics. Notes to the Teacher are available in the *Video* package, and Student Activity Sheets can be downloaded from the ***WorldView* Companion Website**.

• **The *WorldView* Companion Website** (www.longman.com/worldview) provides a variety of teaching support, including Video Activity Sheets and supplemental reading material.

Unit contents

Each of the units in *WorldView* has seven closely linked sections:
• **Getting started:** a communicative opening exercise that introduces target vocabulary
• **Listening/Reading:** a functional conversation or thematic passage that introduces target grammar
• **Grammar focus:** an exercise sequence that allows students to focus on the new grammar point and to solidify their learning
• **Pronunciation:** stress, rhythm, and intonation practice based on the target vocabulary and grammar
• **Speaking:** an interactive speaking task focused on student production of target vocabulary, grammar, and functional language
• **Writing:** a personalized writing activity that stimulates student production of target vocabulary and grammar
• **Conversation to go:** a concise reminder of the grammar functional language introduced in the unit

Course length

With its flexible format and course components, *WorldView* responds to a variety of course needs, and is suitable for 35 to 45 hours of classroom instruction. Each unit can be easily expanded by using bonus activities from the *Teacher's Edition*, reproducible activities available in the *Teacher's Resource Book*, linked lessons from the *WorldView Video* program, and supplementary reading assignments in the *WorldView Companion Website*.

Scope and Sequence

GRAMMAR FOCUS	PRONUNCIATION	SPEAKING	WRITING
will/won't for future	Contractions with will	Predicting the future	Predict an episode of a soap opera, a news story, or the result of a sports event
Future real conditional (If + simple present + will)	Intonation in future real conditional sentences	Talking about future possibilities	Propose ideas for an advertisement to sell a product
Verbs + gerund; verbs + infinitive	Weak forms of to in infinitives; blended "wanna" for want to	Talking about changing habits	Write a letter describing recent changes in your work or personal life
used to and would	Blended pronunciation of used to ("useta")	Comparing past and present trends	Compare your lifestyle with that of your parents when they were your age
Passive (simple present)	Syllabic consonants (cotton, metal) with no vowel sound	Describing where things come from	Describe a special item you bought on a trip or that someone gave you
so, too, neither, (not) either	Number of syllables and word stress patterns	Talking about favorite movies	Describe what kinds of movies you and a friend or relative like and don't like
Modals: Could you, Would you, Would you mind . . .? for polite requests	Weak forms and linking: could you, would you	Making or responding to requests	Describe an annoying situation and what you did about it
Passive (simple past)	Stress and rhythm in passive sentences	Describing a crime	Write a newspaper article about a real or imaginary crime
Review: verbs for likes/dislikes followed by gerund and/or infinitive	Consonant clusters (stand, play, sports)	Discussing work and after-work activities	Write an email about your efforts to balance work and play
Relative clauses with that, which, who, where	Stress in nouns and noun phrases	Describing people, places, and things	Describe different kinds of technical equipment you would like to have
It's + adjective/noun + infinitive to express opinion	Different pronunciations of /t/ linked to a following word	Talking about relationships	Write an email giving advice about a marriage problem
Verbs with two objects	Weak pronunciation of object pronouns	Talking about money	Write a letter explaining how you would spend one million dollars
Review: should/shouldn't, could, ought to for advice	Reduced forms of should/could/ought to	Giving advice	Write a letter giving advice to a friend or relative about a problem
Present unreal conditional (If + simple past + would + verb)	Contracted and weak forms of would in rapid speech	Talking about imaginary situations	Write an invitation to a party

Mumbai Soap

Vocabulary Topics for TV soap operas
Grammar *will/won't* for future
Speaking Predicting the future

Lesson A

Getting started

1 Do you watch soap operas on TV? Which is your favorite one?

2 Which five topics do you most often see in soap operas? Check (✓) the topics in the box.

crime	death	family life	greed	illness
marriage	misfortune	money	power	romance

3 *PAIRS.* Compare your answers.

Reading

4 Look at the photos of scenes from a television soap opera from India. Which topics in Exercise 2 do you think the soap opera is about?

5 Read Part One of the soap opera and check your answers to Exercise 4.

....

PART ONE

"NINA, you can't leave me," cries Sanjay, and Nina thinks her heart will break. She thinks about the soccer match in Mumbai where she met Sanjay. She knows her parents will never accept this man with no money or family connections. And she loves and respects her parents. They've told her, "Go to London and stay with our family there. You'll soon forget Sanjay."

6 How do you think Nina will solve her problem? Choose *a*, *b*, or *c* and say why.

a. She'll run away and marry Sanjay.
b. She'll stay in India, but she'll stop seeing Sanjay.
c. She'll go to London.

7   **Read Part Two of the story and check your predictions.**

PART TWO

"WILL we see each other again?" asks Sanjay. "Of course," promises Nina. "And I'll email every day." Her emails tell Sanjay all about her life in London and her acting classes. But they don't mention Ravi, a family friend also living in London. "Marry me, Nina," Ravi says. Nina asks for time to think. The next day she gets a call offering her an important role in a popular British soap opera. When Sanjay finds out about this, he writes, "I know you're happy in London. Please forget me." "No!" cries Nina.

8   **What do you think will happen next? Choose *a*, *b*, or *c* and say why.**

   a. Nina will go back to India and marry Sanjay.
   b. She'll accept the job and tell Sanjay about Ravi.
   c. She'll accept the job and stay in London.

9   **Read Part Three of the story and check your predictions.**

PART THREE

FIVE years later, Sanjay turns on the TV in his Liverpool hotel room. Tomorrow he will play soccer for India. He knows Nina is in London, but he doesn't think he'll see her. He still remembers her last email: "I won't marry anyone else, but I must stay in London. It's not just the job . . . it's also my family. I'll always love you." Sanjay can hear her voice. He turns in surprise and sees her on the TV screen. "She's as beautiful as ever. Is it too late?" he asks himself.

Grammar focus

1 **Study the examples with *will* and *won't*.**

***Will* for future**	***Will* for predictions**
(+) I'll (will) always **love** you.	She **thinks** her heart **will break**.
(–) I **won't** (will not) **marry** anyone else.	He **doesn't think** he'll **see** her again.
(?) Will you **remember** me?	**Do** you **think** it **will be** too late?

2 **Look at the examples again. Underline the correct words to complete the explanations in the chart.**

***will/won't* for future predictions**
Use *will* or *won't* to talk about something that you **think / know** is going to happen.
Use *don't think* + subject + *will* to talk about something you think **is / isn't** going happen.

Grammar Reference page 146

3 **Complete the text with *will* or *won't* and a verb from the box. Use contractions when possible.**

call   get   go   happen   marry   meet   recognize   speak

What do you think **(1)** __will happen__ in the final episode of "Mumbai Soap"?

I think Sanjay **(2)** _____ Nina's phone number from a mutual friend. He

(3) _____ her, but he'll hear a man's voice and he **(4)** _____ **(not)**.

But Nina and Sanjay **(5)** _____ again. I think Nina **(6)** _____ to

Liverpool to watch the soccer game with friends. I don't think she **(7)** _____

Sanjay at first. But he'll be the hero of the game. Do you think Nina **(8)** _____

Sanjay at last?

Pronunciation

4 🎧 **Listen. Notice the pronunciation of the contracted and weak forms of *will*.**

I'll always	I'll always love you.
you'll forget	You'll forget me.
it'll be	Do you think it'll be too late?
her heart will break	She thinks her heart will break.

5 🎧 **Listen again and repeat.**

Speaking

6 *BEFORE YOU SPEAK.* **What do you think will happen in the final episode of "Mumbai Soap"? Write your notes in the chart.**

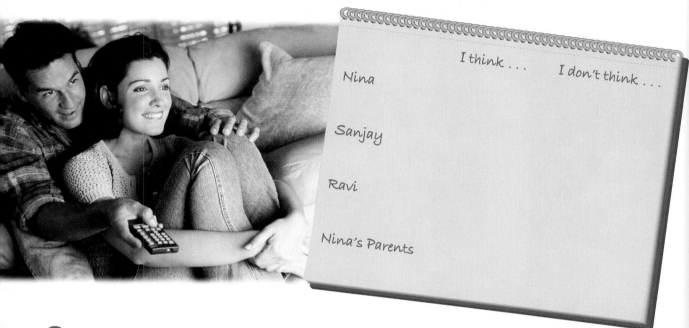

I think . . .   I don't think . . .

Nina

Sanjay

Ravi

Nina's Parents

7 *GROUPS OF 4.* **Take turns telling each other how you predict the soap opera will end.**

Family life is very important to Nina, so I think she'll tell her parents about Sanjay. I don't think they'll be happy . . .

8 Listen to the summary of the last episode and check your predictions.

Writing

9 **Write a note to a friend. Make predictions about one of these things. Use *will* or *won't*.**

- What will happen in the next episode of your favorite TV program?
- What will be the result of the next big sports event in your area?
- What will be the main story in tomorrow's newspapers?

CONVERSATION TO GO

A: **Will** you **ever** see her again?
B: No, I **don't think** I **will**.

16 The message behind the ad

Vocabulary Adjectives used in advertisements
Grammar Future factual conditional (*If* + simple present + *will*)
Speaking Talking about future possibilities

Getting started

1 Underline the best adjectives to complete the sentences about the products.

1. Medallion is a **delicious** / **shiny** new coffee. Try it—you'll love it.
2. You'll have **shiny** / **fresh** hair every time you use Gloss shampoo. So, for **reliable** / **healthy-looking** hair, use Gloss today.
3. Sunease sunscreen will keep your skin **fast** / **safe** from sunburn all through the day. And it keeps your skin **delicious** / **soft**, too!
4. Drink **safe** / **fresh** Sundew orange juice for breakfast—the **clean** / **healthy** way to start your day.
5. Now Lux-Clean laundry soap is even better. Your clothes will always be **clean** / **delicious** and very **reliable** / **soft**.
6. If you dream of working with a **soft** / **fast** and totally **healthy** / **reliable** computer, try the new VMC laptop today.

2 *PAIRS.* Compare your answers.

Reading

3 Read the article about viewers' reactions to television ads. Are their reactions positive or negative?

Talking Back to Ads

ADS ON TV ARE A ONE-WAY STREET – they talk and we listen. But, does it have to be that way? Last week, we encouraged television viewers to talk back to advertisers about how people in the ads are portrayed. If you believe you can make a difference, read what some people had to say about most TV ads.

Yoko, a college student, said, "Advertisers seem to think that if they show thin, attractive people, everyone will want to buy what they're selling, whether it's a car, a soft drink, or perfume. I like to see ads that have real people in them, not just good-looking models."

Roger, a computer analyst, is especially worried about ads that target young children. "I have an eleven-year-old son, and I don't want him to think that physical appearance is the most important thing in life. A lot of TV ads tell kids that if they don't wear certain clothes, they won't be popular with other kids."

If you call or write to the advertiser and the TV network every time you see an ad that offends you, you will be able to change the way advertisers portray people. Let advertisers know what you think!

4 Read the article again and answer the questions.

1. What does the article encourage people to do? Why?
2. What kind of people would Yoko like to see on TV?
3. Why is Roger especially worried about ads that target young children?

Listening

5 *GROUPS OF 3.* Describe an advertisement you've seen recently. What was the message of the ad?

The new ad for Super-Fresh shampoo shows beautiful women having a great time dancing. The message is, "Use this shampoo and you'll be beautiful and happy."

6 Listen to the interview with an advertising executive. Check (✓) the photos of the products in Exercise 1 that they talk about.

7 Listen again and answer the questions.

1. What kind of people do they use in car advertisements?
2. Which products often use families in their advertisements?
3. Why is humor a good thing to use in ads?

Grammar focus

1 **Study the examples of the future real conditional.**

> **(+) If** you **buy** this car, you**'ll meet** a beautiful woman.
> People **will remember** the ad **if** it**'s** funny.
> **(–) If** you **use** this sunscreen, your kids **won't get** sunburned.
> You **won't** regret it **if** you **try** our product.
> **(?)** What **will happen if** I **buy** this car?

2 **Look at the examples again. Underline the correct word or phrase to complete the rules in the chart.**

> **Future real conditional**
>
> Use the future real conditional to talk about things that may or may not happen.
>
> The verb in the *if* clause is in the **simple present / future**.
>
> When the *if* clause comes first, it **is / isn't** usually followed by a comma (,).

> *Grammar Reference page 146*

3 **Complete the sentences with the correct form of the verbs in parentheses.**

1. You <u>'ll lose</u> **(lose)** weight quickly if you <u>don't eat</u> **(not eat)** sweet things.
2. If you _____ **(try)** this lemonade, you _____ **(not want)** to drink anything else.
3. If you _____ **(use)** Gloss shampoo, your hair _____ **(look)** really shiny.
4. You _____ **(have)** more energy if you _____ **(eat)** lots of fresh fruit.
5. If the machine _____ **(break)**, we _____ **(repair)** it free of charge.
6. If you _____ **(drink)** Vita-mint, you _____ **(have)** lots of energy all day long.
7. You _____ **(not feel)** so tired if you _____ **(exercise)** at our gym every day.
8. Your skin _____ **(be)** softer if you _____ **(wash)** with Callon soap every day.

Pronunciation

4 🎧 **Listen. Notice the intonation in these conditional sentences.**

If you buy this car, you'll meet a beautiful woman.

If the ad is funny, people will remember it.

If you use this sunscreen, your kids won't get sunburned.

If you try our product, you won't regret it.

5 🎧 **Listen again and repeat.**

Speaking

6 *BEFORE YOU SPEAK.* **Look at the advertisements above. Who are the advertisers "targeting" (trying to sell the products to)? Make notes.**

- young, middle-aged, or older people?
- single or married people?
- men, women, or both?
- people with children?

7 *PAIRS.* **Discuss each ad. Who are the advertisers targeting? What is the message behind each ad?**

I think they're targeting . . .
To me, the message is, "If you use this . . ."

8 **Report on the messages. Do your classmates agree?**

Writing

9 **You work for an advertising agency. Write a paragraph with ideas for an ad to sell a product you use and like. Use the future real conditional.**

CONVERSATION TO GO

A: If you **buy** this car, you**'ll get** a lot of attention.
B: Especially from my mechanic!

Unit 15 Mumbai Soap

8 *BEFORE YOU SPEAK.* Read the TV guide. What do you think will happen on Wednesday? What do you think will happen on Friday?

TV GUIDE - WEEK IN REVIEW

Final week of
Love Me or Leave Me

MONDAY	TUESDAY	WEDNESDAY	THURSDAY	FRIDAY
Five days before their wedding, Linda and Evan have a huge fight and break up.	Linda visits an old boyfriend in San Francisco, and Evan goes fishing.	Evan an[...] make[...] are [...] th[...]e.	Linda and Evan go to the wedding rehearsal. The radio station BRMB is there to broadcast the wedding and interview them live before and after their wedding.	Tune in for the grand finale – the final episode of "Love Me or Leave Me."

---

9 🎧 Listen to the model conversation and look at the photos.

10 *PAIRS.* Share your predictions.

Unit 16   The message behind the ad

11 🎧 Listen to the model conversation.

12 *BEFORE YOU SPEAK.* Choose a product and write an advertising slogan using an *if* clause.

13 *GROUPS OF 3.* Share your slogan with two classmates. Who came up with the best slogan? The funniest slogan? The most creative slogan?

UNIT 17

Willpower

Vocabulary Phrasal verbs
Grammar Verbs + gerund; verbs + infinitive
Speaking Talking about changing habits

Getting started

1 *Willpower* is the ability to control your mind and body in order to achieve something. Match the phrasal verbs about willpower with the correct definitions. You will use one definition twice.

Phrasal verbs	Definitions
1. I heard that you **took up** yoga recently. _d_ 2. I can't believe she **threw away** all the chocolates! ___ 3. I finally **gave up** drinking coffee in the afternoon. ___ 4. You'll have to **cut down on** desserts if you want to lose weight. ___ 5. I **keep on** going to the gym every day, even though I hate it. ___ 6. Every day she has a new excuse to **get out of** exercising. ___ 7. Many people **cut back on** carbohydrates to lose weight. ___ 8. I **turned down** their dinner invitation because I'm on a diet. ___	a. stopped doing something that you did regularly before b. did not accept an offer or opportunity c. continue to do something d. started doing a particular activity e. avoid doing something that you should do f. put something in the trash g. reduce the amount, number, or size of something

2 *PAIRS.* Take turns telling each other about something you've begun doing or cut back on recently. Use some of the phrasal verbs in Exercise 1.

Last summer, I took up tennis. I tried to cut down on sweets, but I just couldn't give up ice cream.

3 *PAIRS.* Discuss these questions.

Which of these things take a lot of willpower?
Which don't take much willpower?

• exercising
• giving up drinking coffee
• getting organized
• giving up watching television
• learning to speak a new language
• learning to play a musical instrument

Reading

4 Take the the quiz to find out how much willpower you have.

Do you have willpower?

Can you do things even if they're difficult? Can you finish what you start? Read each situation and circle a, b, or c.

1 You have stopped eating sweets, but today you're home alone and you're hungry. There's a box of chocolates in the kitchen. Do you decide to:
a. eat all the chocolates but not buy any more?
b. throw away the whole box and give up eating sweets forever?
c. eat one or two and then throw away the rest?

2 You love buying new things, but you already have too much charged on your credit card. You realize you need to cut down on spending. Will you:
a. try to shop only when there are sales?
b. quit shopping until all your bills are paid?
c. only shop when you really need to buy something?

3 You have a bad temper and your family dislikes going places with you. Do you decide to:
a. not worry about how your family feels?
b. take an anger management course and learn to control your temper?
c. practice not losing your temper, but if you do, be sure to apologize?

4 You don't enjoy exercising, but you want to get in shape. You take up jogging. One day as you start jogging, you meet a good friend who invites you for coffee. Will you:
a. stop to have a cup of coffee with your friend?
b. give an excuse to get out of having coffee and keep on jogging?
c. promise to meet him or her in five minutes and only jog around the park once?

5 Count the number of *a*'s, *b*'s, and *c*'s you circled. Then turn to page 137 to find out how much willpower you have.

6 *PAIRS.* Tell your partner your results on the willpower quiz. Do you agree or disagree with the results? Why? What can you do to have more willpower?

Grammar focus

1 Study the examples of verbs followed by gerunds and infinitives.

Verbs + gerund	Verbs + infinitive
(+) He **kept on** running.	I **want to eat** something.
(–) I don't **enjoy doing** exercise.	You **don't need to have** a cup of coffee.
(?) Did you **give up drinking** soda?	Did he **learn to control** his temper?

2 Look at the verbs in the box. Find these verbs in the quiz in Exercise 4. Put them into the correct column in the chart.

decide	give up	cut down on	need	quit
dislike	practice	learn	enjoy	get out of
want	take up	keep on	stop	promise

Verbs followed by gerund	Verbs followed by infinitive
give up	decide

Grammar Reference page 147

3 Complete the paragraph with the correct form of the verbs in parentheses.

Before I went to Mexico on vacation, I decided _____ Spanish classes.
    1. (take)

I needed _____ work early to get to class. The class was hard, so I quit
        2. (leave)

_____ it and got some Spanish cassettes. I didn't enjoy _____ to
  3. (take)   **4. (listen)**

the cassettes, but I didn't want the _____ _____ Spanish. I kept on
                            5. (give up)   **6. (learn)**

_____ to study, but I didn't have enough time. So I finally stopped
  7. (try)

_____ . When I got to Mexico, I found that many people there speak
  8. (try)

some English, and they were happy to practice _____ English with me!
                                              9. (speak)

Pronunciation

4 🎧 **Listen. Notice the weak pronunciation of *to* in the verbs followed by infinitives and the disappearing /t/ sound in *want to* ("wanna").**

I want to lose weight.

I need to get more exercise.

I learned to play tennis.

But then I wanted to eat more.

I want to eat less.

I decided to stop eating chocolate.

I decided to go jogging every day.

And I needed to lose more weight.

5 🎧 **Listen again and repeat.**

Speaking

6 *GROUPS OF 3.* **Take turns. Toss a coin (one side of the coin = move one space, the other side of the coin = move two spaces). When you land on a space, use the cues to make a sentence. If your sentence is correct, stay on the space. If it is incorrect, move back to where you started your turn. The first person to reach FINISH wins.**

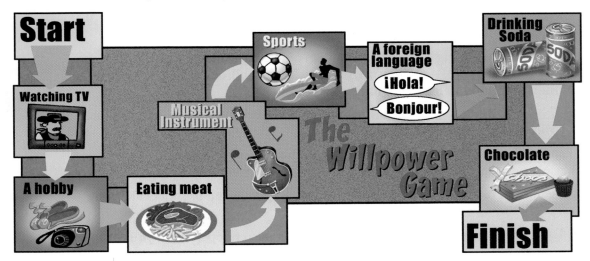

Writing

7 **Write a letter to a friend. Describe recent changes you have made either in your work life or personal life, including things you have given up, cut back on, or taken up. You can use your imagination. Use verbs + gerund, verbs + infinitive, and some of the phrasal verbs from this unit.**

CONVERSATION TO GO

A: Could I have a piece of your chocolate?
B: Sure. But didn't you quit eating chocolate?
A: No. I only gave up buying chocolate.

UNIT 18

Lesson A

Wave of the future

Vocabulary Words related to new trends
Grammar *Used to* and *would*
Speaking Comparing past and present trends

A

Getting started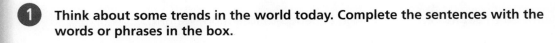

1 **Think about some trends in the world today. Complete the sentences with the words or phrases in the box.**

alternative medicine	genetic engineering	hybrid cars	instant messaging
~~renewable resources~~	telecommuting	vegetarianism	

1. People are looking for ways to use <u>renewable resources</u>, like solar energy or windmills, for their energy needs.

2. _____ is quickly replacing the telephone as an easy way to communicate, especially among teenagers.

3. Many restaurants have responded to the trend toward _____ and serve meals using vegetables and grains, but no meat.

4. Instead of traveling to an office, many people are turning to _____. They use phones, faxes, mail, and the Internet to do their jobs without leaving home.

5. _____ use both gasoline and electricity. They are considered friendly to the environment.

6. Acupuncture, herbal remedies, and other traditional Chinese practices have become popular forms of _____ in the U.S.

7. Scientists use _____ to alter agricultural products like corn.

2 *PAIRS.* **Compare your answers. Are these trends also happening in your country?**

3 **Look at the photos. Which of the trends in Exercise 1 does each one show?**

4 *GROUPS OF 3.* **Discuss these questions.**

What's one advantage and one disadvantage of each trend in Exercise 1?
Which trends do you think will most likely become widespread?
Which trends will die out?

A: *Telecommuting has the advantage that you don't have to waste time getting to and from work.*
B: *I agree, but a disadvantage is that you have no personal contact with your coworkers.*

Listening

5 🎧 **Listen to the first part of the conversation between Beth and Han-su. What's Beth's job?**

6 🎧 **Listen to the second part of the conversation. Write *T* (true) or *F* (false) after each statement.**

According to Beth . . .

1. people used to think that regular books and magazines would disappear. T
2. telecommuting is not very common.
3. people know we need to use renewable resources.
4. people don't worry about wasting energy.
5. solar panels will soon be on every home and business.
6. SUVs are a wave of the future.

7 *PAIRS.* **Compare your answers.**

Grammar focus

1 Look at the examples. Which of these express a past action?
Which of these express a past state? Write *PA* or *PS* next to each one.

> **(+)** People **used to** think that regular books would disappear.
> We **would** get up, get dressed, and go to our work places.
> My sister **used to** drive a small car. Now she drives an SUV.
>
> **(–)** People **didn't use to** worry about wasting energy.
> A few years ago, people **wouldn't** stop talking about e-books.
>
> **(?) Did** she **use to** drive a large car?

2 Look at the examples again. Fill in the blanks with *used to* or *would* to
complete the rules in the chart.

Used to and *would*
Use both _____ and _____ for repeated past actions.
Use _____ only to talk about a past state (with *be, have, like, hate* . . .).
NOTE: *Would* usually needs a time reference *(every day, when I was a child)*. *Used to* is more common at the beginning of a narrative. Use *would* in later sentences, especially to avoid repetition.

Grammar Reference page 147

3 Make sentences with a similar meaning, using the correct form of *used to*.

1. When my brother was younger, he worked twelve hours every day.
   When my brother was younger, he used to work twelve hours every day.

2. I hated sports when I was in school, but now I'm a big soccer fan.

3. In the past, my boss drove her car to work every day,
   but now she uses public transportation.

4. Telecommuting was not very popular years ago, but
   now many people work from home.

5. Tania is a vegetarian now. She ate meat at least
   once a day when she was younger.

6. Beto drives a hybrid car now. He had a regular
   car before.

7. When she was younger, Kim went to the beach
   every weekend.

4 In which sentences from Exercise 3 could you also
use *would*?

Pronunciation

5 🎧 **Listen. Notice that *used to* and *use to* are pronounced the same way: "use**ta**."**

used to	She used to drive a small car.
use to	Did you use to work in an office?
didn't use to	I didn't use to like vegetables.

6 🎧 **Listen again and repeat.**

Speaking

7 *BEFORE YOU SPEAK.* **Think about your past and current habits. Complete the sentences.**

8 *PAIRS.* **Take turns telling each other about your past and present habits. Ask follow-up questions.**

A: I used to eat a lot of chocolate.
B: Really? Did you have chocolate every day?
A: Yes, I would.

9 **Tell the class about one of your partner's habits.**

Writing

10 **Compare your lifestyle with that of your parents when they were your age. What is different? What things were better or worse? Use *used to* and *would*.**

1. Eating habits
   I used to eat a lot of _____.
   I would buy _____.
   Now I _____ all the time.
   _____.

2. Commuting
   I used to go to school/ work by _____
   _____ (form of transportation).
   I would spend_____(amount of time) getting ready and traveling.
   Now I _____
   _____.

3. Other _____.
   I used to _____
   _____
   I would _____.
   _____
   Now _____
   _____.

CONVERSATION TO GO

A: I used to live in the city, but last year we moved to the countryside.
B: I did the opposite. I used to have a house in the suburbs, and I'd drive two hours to work every day.

UNIT 19

Made in the U.S.A.

Vocabulary Materials; possessions
Grammar Passive (simple present)
Speaking Describing where things come from

Getting started

1 Look at the pictures of items you can buy at Fisherman's Wharf in San Francisco. Match each item with the material.

1. cotton __G__   2. glass _____   3. gold _____   4. leather _____

5. pewter _____   6. lycra _____   7. silver _____   8. wood _____

2 🎧 Listen and check your answers. Then listen again and repeat.

3 *PAIRS.* Take turns asking and answering the questions.

What things do you typically buy of wood or glass?

Do you prefer silver or gold jewelry? Why?

Do you prefer cotton or polyester clothing? Why?

What kinds of leather clothes or accessories do you like?

What is your most treasured possession? What material is it made of?

Visit Fisherman's Wharf

with its spectacular view of the bay and handicrafts from all over the world

Listening

4 🎧 **Listen to Marcela and Peter, tourists at Fisherman's Wharf in San Francisco. Complete the chart with information on the items they talk about.**

Item	Material	Country of origin	Price
mirror			

5 🎧 **Listen again. Circle the picture of the item Peter buys.**

6 *PAIRS.* **Why does Peter buy it?**

Pronunciation

7 🎧 **Listen. Notice that the sound /n/ or /l/ can form a syllable without a vowel sound.**

cotton   wooden   didn't

metal   sandals   candlesticks

8 🎧 **Listen. Notice how the words with these sounds are pronounced in the sentences.**

They didn't buy the cotton shirt.   They didn't buy the wooden boxes.

They didn't buy the sandals.   They didn't buy the metal candlesticks.

9 🎧 **Listen again and repeat.**

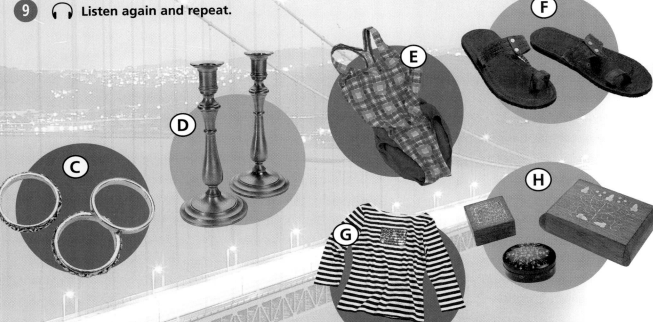

Grammar focus

1 **Study the examples of the active and passive voice.**

Active voice	Passive voice
They make the mirrors in Holland by hand.	The mirrors **are handmade** in Holland.
Artists hand-paint the mirrors.	The mirrors are hand-painted by artists.
The big stores sell it for at least $75.	It's sold in the big stores for at least $75.
Where do they make it?	Where **is** it **made**?

2 **Look at the examples again. Circle _a_ or _b_ to answer the questions.**

Simple present passive

In the passive sentences, which is more important?

a. the people who make, sell, or buy things   b. the things that they make, sell, or buy

How do you form the simple present passive?

a. _have_ + the past participle   b. _be_ + the past participle

> *Grammar Reference page 147*

3 **Rewrite the sentences in the passive. Do not mention the agent (the person or thing that does the action) unless it is necessary to understand the sentence.**

1. We call rugs from Turkey, Iran, and Pakistan Oriental rugs.

   Rugs from Turkey, Iran, and Pakistan are called Oriental rugs.

2. Cosmetics companies use fish scales to make lipstick.

3. The U.S. imports most of its electronics from Japan.

4. Both the medical industry and the photography industry use silver.

5. Swiss companies manufacture most of the gold watches in the world.

6. Factories in Canada produce most of the foreign cars sold in the U.S.

7. Food companies add preservatives to food to make it last longer.

8. The supply of materials affects the price of the product.

Speaking

4 Find someone in the class who has something with him or her today, or who is wearing something, made of the materials listed below. Complete the chart with the answers. Find out other details.

A: Are you wearing anything made of cotton?
B: Yes, my jacket is made of cotton.
A: Is it handmade?
B: No.
A: Is it imported?

Person	Material	Object	Handmade?	Imported?
	cotton			
	gold			
	leather			
	silver			
	wood			

5 *PAIRS.* Take turns telling each other about the results of your survey.

Min-ja's jacket is made of cotton. It's not handmade. It's made in Korea.

6 Take a poll of the class. Find out what things people have that are made of cotton, gold, leather, silver, and wood.

Writing

7 Write a paragraph about something special that you bought on a trip or that someone gave you. Say what it is made of, who made it, and where it was made. Use the passive voice.

CONVERSATION TO GO

A: Did you make that ring?
B: Yes, I did.
A: What's it made of?
B: Silver.

UNIT 20

Lesson A

At the movies

Vocabulary Types of movies
Grammar *so, too, neither, (not) either*
Speaking Talking about favorite movies

Getting started

1 Match the comments about movies with the words in the box.

> a) an action movie b) an animated film c) a comedy
>
> d) a drama   e) a horror movie f) a martial arts film g) a musical
>
> h) a science fiction movie i) a thriller j) a western

1. It was very intense. The ending was totally surprising. __i__
2. I laughed all the time. _____
3. I loved the music and the dancing. _____
4. It was really scary. I had to close my eyes every five minutes. _____
5. There were lots of fights between cowboys. _____
6. It's set in the future, when computers run the world. _____
7. The hero fought off a whole army with his bare hands. _____
8. It's full of exciting scenes, with lots of explosions and car chases. _____
9. It's a very emotional story about a man who lived alone on an island. _____
10. It's a computer-animated comedy about friendly monsters. _____

90

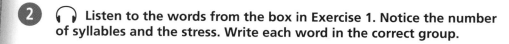

Pronunciation

2 🎧 **Listen to the words from the box in Exercise 1. Notice the number of syllables and the stress. Write each word in the correct group.**

⬤ ○	○ ⬤ ○	○ ○ ⬤ ○	⬤ ○ ○ ○
drama			

3 🎧 **Listen and check your answers. Then listen again and repeat.**

4 *PAIRS.* **Use the words from Exercise 1 to say at least two things about each of the movies in the posters.**

Listening

5 *PAIRS.* **Guess the answer to each question.**

1. Which of these movies made the most money at the box office?
   a. *Star Wars*
   b. *E.T.*
   c. *Titanic*

2. Which of these movies was the most expensive to make?
   a. *Lord of the Rings*
   b. *Star Wars*
   c. *Titanic*

6 🎧 **Listen to the interview and check your guesses.**

7 🎧 **Listen again. Write *T* (true) or *F* (false) after each statement. If the statement is false, write the correct information.**

1. The interviewer and the guest both think *Star Wars* is one of the best animated films ever made.

2. Both the interviewer and the guest were surprised at *Titanic's* success.

3. Not many movies have mistakes in them.

4. The most frequent mistake in movies involves the clothes the actors and extras wear.

Lesson B

Grammar focus

1 **Study the examples of additions with *so, too, neither,* and *not either*.**

> The editors are upset, and **so** are the directors.
> The editors are upset, and the directors are, **too**.
> I didn't know that, and **neither** did the fans.
> I didn't know that, and the fans did**n't either**.

2 **Look at the examples again. Underline the correct information to complete the rules in the chart.**

> **Additions: *so, too, neither, (not) either***
>
> Additions always use a form of *be,* an auxiliary verb (such as *have* or *do*), or a modal (such as *can, should,* or *will*). The verb tense in the addition must match the verb tense in the first sentence.
>
> Use *so* or *too* if the addition follows **an affirmative / a negative** statement.
>
> Use *neither* or *not either* if the addition follows **an affirmative / a negative** statement.
>
> In additions with *so* and *neither,* the subject comes **after / before** the verb.

> *Grammar Reference page 147*

3 **Rewrite the sentences using *so, too, either,* or *neither*. Remember to use commas correctly.**

1. Both Silvia and Pedro are movie experts.

   Silvia is a movie expert, and so is Pedro.

2. Bruce and David can't go to the movies tonight.

3. Frank and Lois were disappointed in the musical they saw.

4. Russell Crowe and Cameron Diaz are famous actors.

5. Two comedies, *All Day Long* and *Mother*, are playing tonight.

6. Yi-Lian and her friend don't like horror movies.

7. Pat and Omar thought the acting was terrible.

8. Alice and Vera didn't like the ending to the thriller.

4 *PAIRS.* **Compare your answers from Exercise 3. If your answers are the same, what other way could you say the same thing?**

Silvia is a movie expert, and Pedro is, too.

Speaking

5 *GROUPS OF 3.* **Take turns asking each other about the kinds of movies you like. What are your favorite movies? Take notes on the survey form.**

A: *Do you like action movies?*
B: *Yes. My favorite action movie is* The Matrix Reloaded.

Movie Madness

	Student 1		Student 2	
	like?	favorite	like?	favorite
action movie				
animated film				
comedy				
drama				
horror movie				
martial arts film				
musical				
science fiction				
thriller				
western				

6 **Report to the class. Tell what you found out about your classmates' taste in movies.**

Senna doesn't like romantic comedies, and neither does Flavia.

Writing

7 **Choose two similar movies (for example, two action movies or two comedies). Write a review comparing the two movies. Give some examples from the movies. Use the additions *so, too, either,* or *neither*.**

CONVERSATION TO GO

A: Terry loves action films, and so does Alex.
B: Well, I don't like them at all, and neither does Dana.

Unit 17 Willpower

1 🎧 Listen to the model conversation.

2 *GROUPS OF 3.* With your group, make up a fictional story. Use at least six verbs from the box plus gerunds or infinitives. Each member of the group contributes at least three sentences to the story.

decide	dislike	enjoy	give up	keep on	learn
need	practice	quit	stop	take up	want

3 Take turns sharing your story with the other groups.

Unit 18 Wave of the future

4 Check (✔) the things your parents used to do in the past. Add two more habits to the list.

Did your parents use to . . .	Name
buy records?	
write long letters to friends and relatives?	
drive a very big car?	
waste electricity?	

5 🎧 Listen to the model conversation.

6 Talk to your classmates. Ask questions until you get "yes" answers to all your questions. Write your classmates' names in the column on the right. Ask follow-up questions.

Unit 19 Made in the U.S.A.

7 **PAIRS.** What are some things you have now that you can try to "sell"? What are they made of? Where are they made? Complete the chart.

Item	Material	Origin
Earrings	Silver and gold	Brazil

8 🎧 Listen to the model conversation.

9 **2 PAIRS.** You and your partner are shopping. Take turns asking the other pair what they sell, what materials the items are made of, and what countries they come from. Which things would you buy? Switch roles with the other pair.

Unit 20 At the movies

10 🎧 Listen to the model conversation.

11 **GROUPS OF 4.** Write the names of three movies (or TV programs) to talk about. Survey your group members about their opinions. Ask follow-up questions to find out what each person especially likes or dislikes about each movie. Take notes in the chart.

12 Tell the class the results of your survey.

Ron didn't like Endless Night, *and neither did John.*

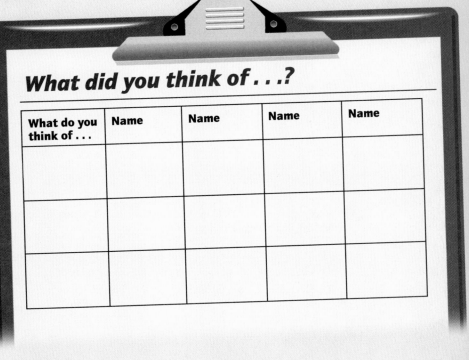

What did you think of . . .?

What do you think of . . .	Name	Name	Name	Name

World of Music 3

You've Got a Friend
Carole King

Songwriter **Carole King** says that You've Got a Friend *is one of only two songs that she created through sheer inspiration. The song is a signature tune for singer James Taylor, a long-time friend of King's.*

Vocabulary

1 *GROUPS OF 3.* **What do you think these phrases or sentences mean? Choose the best answer.**

1. You're down and troubled and need some love and care.
   a. You fell and need help to get up again.
   b. You're sad and in need of a friend.
   c. You don't feel well and need medicine.

2. If the sky above you grows dark
   a. It will get dark soon
   b. If the day gets dark
   c. If things don't go right for you

3. Keep your head together.
   a. Get close to me.
   b. Stay calm.
   c. Avoid an accident.

4. They'll desert you.
   a. They'll stay with you.
   b. They'll trick you.
   c. They'll forget about you.

Listening

2 🎧 **Listen to "You've Got a Friend," by Carole King. What is the main idea of the song?**

   a. The singer is offering her friendship to somebody.
   b. The singer is promising to visit someone.
   c. The singer is sad and needs a friend to help her.

3 🎧 **Listen again and complete the lyrics on page 97.**

You've Got a Friend

When you're down and troubled
and you need some love and care
and _____, _____ is going right.
Close your _____ and think of me
and soon I will be there
to brighten up even your _____ night.

You just call out my name,
and you know wherever I am
I'll come running to see you _____.
Winter, spring, summer, or fall,
all you _____ ____ do is call
and I'll be there.
You've got a friend.

If the sky above you
grows dark and full of _____
and that old north ____ begins to blow
Keep your head together and _____
my name out loud
Soon you'll hear me knocking at
your _____.

You just call out my name,
and you know wherever I am
I'll come running, running, yeah, yeah
to see you _____.
Winter, spring, summer, or fall
all you have to do is call
and I'll be there, yes, I will.

Now, ain't it good to know that you've
got a friend
when ____ can be so cold?
They'll _____ you, yes and desert you.
And _____ your soul if you let them.
Ah, but don't you let them.

You just call out my name,
and you know wherever I am
I'll come running, running, yeah, yeah
to see you _____.
_____, spring, _____, or fall,
all you have to do is _____.
And, I'll be there, yes, I will.
You've got a friend.
You've got a friend. Yeah, baby.
You've got a friend.
Ain't it good to know you've got
a friend.
Ain't it good to know you've got
a friend.
Oh, yeah now.
You've got a friend.
Oh yeah.
You've got a friend.

Speaking

4 **GROUPS OF 3.** Discuss these questions. Use lines from the song to
explain your answer.

1. When does the singer think a friend is especially useful?
2. How strong are the singer's feelings towards her friend?

How polite are you?

Vocabulary Phrasal verbs with *turn, switch, go*
Grammar Modals: *Could you, Would you, Would you mind* for polite requests
Speaking Making or responding to requests

Lesson A

Getting started

1 Complete the sentences with the word or words in the box.
You will use some words more than once.

down	~~off~~	on	up	over to

1. I hate it when my alarm goes ___off___ in the morning.

2. That music is too loud. Could you turn it _____, please?

3. Can you turn _____ the lights? I can't see what I'm reading.

4. Please turn _____ all cell phones in the aircraft now.

5. I love that song. Can you turn _____ the volume, please?

6. Would you mind switching _____ Channel 13? I want to
watch that Japanese movie.

2 *PAIRS.* **Compare your answers.**

3 *PAIRS.* **Talk about the things you usually turn on when you get home
at night. Think about your TV, computer, lights, etc. What do you turn
on first, second, etc.?**

When I get home, the first thing I turn on is the lights. Then I always . . .

Reading

4 🎧 Listen to some noises and say what they are. How do you feel about them?

5 *PAIRS.* Discuss these questions. Are you a noisy person? If so, when? Do you feel comfortable asking people to stop making noise?

6 Read the situations in "Excuse me . . ." Circle your answers to the questions.

7 *PAIRS.* Discuss your answers. Which answers are most polite? Which are rude?

"Excuse me . . ."

1 You're on a bus. The person next to you is playing loud music. What do you say?

   A "Would you mind turning your music down, please?"
   B "Driver! Can you tell this guy that it's illegal to play music on the bus?"
   C "You're being very rude."

2 You're on a train. The passenger behind you is kicking your seat. What do you say?

   A "Could you stop doing that, please? I can't concentrate."
   B "Conductor! He's kicking my chair!"
   C "Stop that now!"

3 It's the middle of the night. Your neighbor's dog is barking. You can't sleep. You . . .

   A call your neighbor and say, "Could you make Mitzy stop barking, please?"
   B call the police and say, "Would you come quickly, there's a dangerous animal next door!"
   C open the window and shout, "Be quiet!"

4 You're having a romantic dinner in a restaurant. A man near you is speaking loudly on his cell phone. What do you say?

   A "Would you mind lowering your voice, please?"
   B "Waiter! Please tell this man to go outside."
   C "We're trying to have a nice, quiet dinner, and you're disturbing us."

Grammar focus

1 **Study the examples of polite requests and responses.**

Would you please turn the music down?	Of course.
Could I **turn** on the TV?	Sure.
Would you **mind lowering** your voice?	No, of course not.
	Not at all.

2 **Look at the examples again. Underline the correct words to complete the rules in the chart.**

Could you / Would you / Would you mind for polite requests

Use *would you* or *could you* + **the gerund / the base form of the verb** to make polite requests.

Use *Would you mind* + **the gerund / the base form of the verb** to make polite requests.

If you answer *No* to a *would you mind* question, you are saying that you **will / won't** do what the person requests.

Grammar Reference page 148

3 **Look at the pictures. Write polite requests and responses for each situation.**

1. A: <u>Would you mind making</u>
   <u>less noise, please?</u>
   B: <u>No, of course not.</u>

2. _____
   _____
   _____

3. _____
   _____
   _____

4. _____
   _____
   _____

5. _____
   _____
   _____

Pronunciation

4 🎧 **Listen. Notice the way the words *would you* and *could you* are linked and blended together: "wouldja" and "couldja."**

Would you   Would you please turn the music down?

                Would you mind lowering your voice?

Could you   Could you please stop doing that?

                Could you make your dog stop barking?

5 🎧 **Listen again and repeat.**

6 *PAIRS.* **Practice the conversations you wrote in Exercise 3.**

Speaking

7 *PAIRS.* **Role-play situations using polite requests. Student A, look at this page. Student B, look at page 142.**

Role-play #1
You left your wallet at home, and you need to borrow money for lunch from Student B, a close friend.

Role-play #2
Student B is your co-worker. Listen and reply.

Role-play #3
You need to stay at home to take care of your sick child. Ask your boss, Student B, for permission to work from home. You will turn on your cell phone so people can call you from work.

Role-play #4
Student B is your neighbor. Listen and reply.

Writing

8 **Look at the quiz in Exercise 6 on page 99. Have you ever been in a situation like any of those? Describe what happened and include the conversation you had with the annoying person.**

CONVERSATION TO GO

A: Could you turn your music down?
B: What did you say?
A: Would you mind turning it down?
B: No, of course not.

UNIT 22

Lesson A

The art of crime

Vocabulary Words related to crime
Grammar Passive (simple past)
Speaking Describing a crime

Getting started

1 Look at the words associated with crime. Complete the chart.

Crime	Criminal	Verb (+ someone or something)	Meaning
robbery	robber		take money or property illegally from a person or place
burglary		burglarize (a place)	enter a building illegally and take money or goods
mugging	mugger		attack and take something from a person
scam	con artist		use a dishonest plan to get money from somebody
shoplifting		shoplift (something)	take goods from a store without paying
theft		steal (something)	take something illegally

2 🎧 Listen and check your answers. Then listen again and repeat.

3 *PAIRS.* Rank the crimes in Exercise 1 in order of seriousness (1 = the most serious, 6 = the least serious).

4 *GROUPS OF 4.* Decide what punishment each type of criminal deserves.

Should the criminal:
- go to prison? (say for how long)
- pay a fine? (say how much)
- do community service?
  (say what kind of service)

A: A bank robber should go to prison for thirty years.
B: Thirty years is too much, especially if no one got hurt.

102

Listening

5 *PAIRS.* **Look at the painting and read the questions. How much do you know about this painting? Discuss your answers with your partner.**

1. It's called the Mona Lisa in English. Do you know what it's called in your language?

2. Who painted it?

3. What happens if you look at the woman's eyes from different angles?

6 🎧 **In 1911, the Mona Lisa disappeared. Listen to the story and match the questions with the answers.**

1. Who had the idea for the theft? __   a. Eduardo de Valfierno

2. Who stole the painting? __   b. rich collectors

3. Who believed the copies were real? __   c. Vincenzo Perugia

7 🎧 **Listen again. Write *T* (true) or *F* (false) after each statement. Correct the false statements.**

1. The Mona Lisa was painted by Michelangelo. F

   The Mona Lisa was painted by Leonardo Da Vinci.

2. The painting was never found.

3. None of the thieves was ever arrested.

4. Six copies of the painting were made.

Grammar focus

1 Study the examples of active and passive sentences and questions.

Active sentences			Passive sentences		
Subject	**Verb**	**Object**	**Subject**	**Verb**	**Agent**
Da Vinci	painted	the Mona Lisa.	The Mona Lisa	**was painted by**	Da Vinci.
Someone	stole	the painting.	The painting	**was stolen**.	
The police	caught	the thieves.	The thieves	**were caught**.	

Passive questions			
Question word	**Auxiliary**	**Subject**	**Past participle (by)**
Who	**was**	the Mona Lisa	**painted by**?
When	**was**	the thieves	**stolen**?
How	**were**	the painting	**caught**?

2 Look at the examples again. Underline the correct information to complete the explanation in the chart.

Simple past passive
Use the **passive / active** when the action is more important than the person or thing that did the action.

Grammar Reference page 148

3 Rewrite the sentences in the passive. Do not mention the agent (the person or thing that did the action) unless it is important or necessary to understand the sentence.

1. They took over $150,000 from the bank.
   Over $150,000 was taken from the bank.

2. Somebody broke into our house last month.

3. Security personnel arrested many shoplifters during the holiday season.

4. They stole my car yesterday.

5. According to legend, con artists sold the Eiffel Tower dozens of times.

6. The police discovered thousands of pirated CDs.

7. People made copies of the movie months before it reached the video stores.

8. Eduardo de Valfierno sold the Mona Lisa six times.

104

Pronunciation

4 🎧 **Listen to the rhythm in these sentences. Notice that the stressed syllable of each important word is long and clear and that unstressed syllables and unimportant words are short and weak.**

How were the **thieves caught**?   **When** was the **paint**ing **stolen**?

Copies of the **paint**ing were **made**.   The **cop**ies were **sold** to **collec**tors.

The **orig**inal was **off**ered to a **deal**er.   The **paint**ing was re**turned** to the museum.

5 🎧 **Listen again and repeat.**

Speaking

6 *PAIRS.* **You're going to read parts of an article about a famous robbery. Student A, look at page 140. Student B, look at page 142. Read the article. Ask and answer questions about the missing information in your article.**

The Great Train Robbery

7 **Tell the story (without looking at pages 140 and 142) of the Great Train Robbery.**

Writing

8 **Write a short newspaper article about a real or imaginary crime that happened recently. Use the passive voice. Include:**

- the type of crime
- where/when it happened
- who it happened to
- whether or not the criminal was arrested

CONVERSATION TO GO

A: When was your car stolen?
B: Last year. The thieves were never caught.

23 A balanced life

Vocabulary Expressions with take
Grammar Review verbs for likes/dislikes followed by gerund and/or infinitive
Speaking Discussing work and after-work activities

Getting started

1 Look at the pictures and read the conversations. Write the expressions with *take* next to the correct definitions in the chart.

Expression with *take*	Definition
1. take part in	participate in an activity
2.	agree to do something
3.	relax
4.	begin something new
5.	arrange to have time away from work
6.	stop and have a rest

Peter didn't come in today. He took the day off, and I promised Liz I would do all this work.

Well, I don't mind helping if you've taken on too much work.

I want to get into really good shape so I can take part in the marathon this fall.

Long-distance running is too intense for me. But I've taken up yoga. I really like it!

I can't stand studying anymore. I'm going to watch TV and take it easy for a while.

I need to take a break, too. I'm sick of working on this report.

2 *PAIRS.* Compare your answers.

3 *PAIRS.* Talk about something you want to *take part in,* something you want to *take up,* or something you want to *take a break from.* Ask and answer follow-up questions.

A: *I want to take up karate.*
B: *Are you sure? It requires a lot of dedication.*

Listening

4 *PAIRS.* **Look at the photo of Marta and Ian and discuss these questions.**
What is happening in the photo?
What are they saying to each other?

5 **Listen to the conversation and answer the questions.**

1. What reason does Ian give for not going to the gym?
2. How does Marta react?
3. What is Ian's real reason for not going?

Grammar focus

1 Study the examples of verbs to express likes and dislikes.

> Marta **likes to go** to the gym, but Ian **likes watching** basketball on TV.
> Marta **hates watching** sports on TV, but she **loves to work out**.
> He **can't stand working out**, so he **doesn't mind staying** in tonight.
> I **love watching** basketball, but I **hate to watch** the games alone.
> Ian **doesn't enjoy exercising**. He **can't stand to go** to the gym.
> She**'s sick of running**. She**'s into doing** yoga now.

2 Look at the examples again. Complete the rules in the chart.

Verbs for likes/dislikes followed by gerunds and/or infinitives
Use the gerund or infinitive after the following verbs: _____, _____, _____, and _____.
Use only the gerund after the following verbs and phrasal verbs: _____, _____, _____, and _____.

> *Grammar Reference page 148*

3 Write sentences using the prompts. Make any necessary changes. Sometimes more than one correct answer is possible.

1. I really / can't stand / exercise

   I really can't stand exercising.

2. I / sick of / be out of shape, / so I / decided to / take up jogging

3. Now that it's light out / at 6:00 A.M., / I / not mind / get up early

4. You / really into/ practice / yoga now?

5. I / enjoy / play tennis, / but after an hour / I / like / take / a break

6. Kate's boyfriend / not like / go / to the gym

Pronunciation

4 🎧 Listen. Notice the groups of consonant sounds.

I ca**n't st**and **pl**aying tennis, but I do**n't mi**nd **sw**imming.

She ha**tes** watching **sports**, but she lo**ves pract**icing yoga.

He li**kes** e**x**ercising, but sometimes he nee**ds** to take a **br**eak.

5 🎧 Listen again and repeat.

Speaking

6 *BEFORE YOU SPEAK.* **What are you willing to do to be physically fit? Check (✔) the things that you are willing to do. Add two more ideas of your own.**

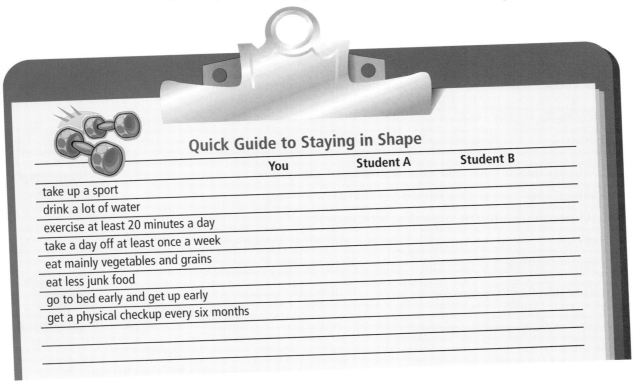

Quick Guide to Staying in Shape

	You	Student A	Student B
take up a sport			
drink a lot of water			
exercise at least 20 minutes a day			
take a day off at least once a week			
eat mainly vegetables and grains			
eat less junk food			
go to bed early and get up early			
get a physical checkup every six months			

7 *GROUPS OF 3.* **Take a survey. Take turns asking one another what you are willing to do. Take notes on the other students' answers.**

A: *Would you take up a sport?*
B: *Yes, why not? I like to play soccer, so I don't mind going to the park on weekends and kicking the ball for a while.*
C: *I really like sports, but I just don't have time right now.*

Writing

8 **Write an email to your friend describing how successful (or unsuccessful) you have been at balancing work and play. Use expressions with *take* and verbs for likes and dislikes.**

CONVERSATION TO GO

A: I don't mind working late once in a while, but I can't stand working late every night.
B: Actually, I like to work overtime because I love getting more money!

Digital age

Vocabulary Technical equipment
Grammar Relative clauses with that, which, who, where
Speaking Describing people, places, and things

Getting started

1 **Look at the names of technical equipment and answer the questions below.**

~~cell phone~~	computer	digital camera	digital TV
laptop	DVD player	printer	scanner

1. Which one lets you make and receive calls? _cell phone_

2. Which two have a screen and a keyboard? _____ _____

3. Which one can put pictures or text on paper? _____

4. Which two make pictures that you can look at on a computer? _____ _____

5. Which one has a screen and a remote control? _____

6. Which one connects to your TV to show movies? _____

SCREEN

2 *PAIRS.* **Compare your answers.**

Pronunciation

REMOTE CONTROL

KEYBOARD

3 🎧 **Listen. Notice the stress. Some of the words in Exercise 1 have two strong syllables.**

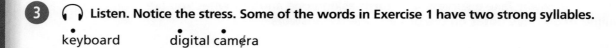

• •
keyboard   digital camera

4 *PAIRS.* **Draw a circle over the strong syllable(s) in each word or phrase. The number (2), indicates that there are two strong syllables.**

cell phone	computer	digital TV (2)	DVD player
laptop	printer	remote control (2)	scanner

5 🎧 **Listen and check your answers. Then listen and repeat.**

6 *GROUPS OF 3.* **Discuss these questions.**

Which of the technical equipment in Exercise 1 do you have?
Which would you like to have?
Which do you think is the most useful?

Reading

7 *PAIRS.* **TVs today are different from the first TVs. Can you describe some differences?**

8 **Read the article about digital television. Write *T* (true) or *F* (false) after each statement.**

1. We can communicate with digital TVs. T
2. Traditional TV pictures use more space than digital pictures.
3. Digital pictures of buildings are sent many times.
4. Traditional television images can be compressed.
5. You can receive digital TV anywhere you are.

9 *PAIRS.* **Read the article again and answer the questions.**

1. What is one thing that we can't do with traditional TV that we can do with digital TV?

2. Why can digital systems send and receive more information?

3. What equipment do you need to get digital TV?

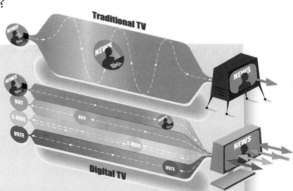

What is digital TV?

In the past, we usually just watched TV. But digital TV is interactive. With digital TV we can easily order things from advertisers, answer quiz questions, or vote on our favorite programs using the remote control. In places where digital TV is very advanced, viewers can get a service that lets them watch any program, whenever they want.

HOW DOES DIGITAL TV WORK?
As you know, a TV studio is a place where they produce TV programs. These programs are "the information" sent from the TV studio to our homes. Traditional TV needs a lot of space to send the information.

With digital systems, the information is in digital form and it can be compressed, so the system can send and receive more information.

Additionally, digital TV systems only send the parts of the picture that change.

So they send a picture of a building once, because it doesn't move. But they send a lot of pictures of people who are walking or cars that are moving around that building.

DO I NEED A SPECIAL TV?
In areas where the service is available, you need either a special TV or a special box that can put the pictures together for your nondigital TV. Then you can watch your favorite program and even "talk" to the station.

Grammar focus

1 **Study the examples of relative clauses.**

> They send a lot of pictures of people **who** are walking.
> They send a lot of pictures of people **that** are walking.
> They only send the parts of the picture **that** change.
> They only send the parts of the picture **which** change.
> A television studio is a place **where** they make programs.

2 **Look at the examples again. Complete the rules in the chart with *that, which, who,* or *where*.**

Relative clauses with *that, which, who,* and *where*
To introduce relative clauses, use:
_____ for places.
_____ or _____ for things.
_____ or _____ for people.

> *Grammar Reference page 148*

3 **Match the beginnings of the sentences on the left with the endings on the right. Then make complete sentences with *that, which, who,* or *where*.**

A pilot is someone who flies planes.

1. ~~A pilot is someone~~
2. A garage is a place
3. A laptop is something
4. A computer analyst is someone
5. A printer is a machine
6. A bank is a place
7. A scanner is something
8. A photographer is a person

a. writes computer programs.
b. takes pictures.
c. ~~flies planes.~~
d. puts words and pictures on paper.
e. transfers information into a computer.
f. you can carry around easily.
g. you park your car.
h. you can get money.

Speaking

4 *GROUPS OF 3.* **Play the Definitions Game. Take turns reading your definitions. Who can guess the word?**

Student A, look at page 138. Student B, look at page 141. Student C, look at page 142.

A: A person who flies planes is . . .
B: A pilot.
A: Correct. You get a point.

Writing

5 **Think about all the technical equipment for work or entertainment that you'd like to have. (It could be something that doesn't exist yet, and the cost is not important.) Write a paragraph describing each piece of equipment. Use relative clauses and some of the vocabulary from this unit.**

CONVERSATION TO GO

A: I want a digital camera **that's** easy to use.
B: I know a place **where** you can buy a really good one.

Unit 21 How polite are you?

1 🎧 Listen to the model conversation.

2 *PAIRS.* Role-play some situations with requests. Student A, use the information below. Student B, look at page 136.

Student A

Role-play #1
You are a teacher. Student B is your student. You are explaining a difficult math problem, but your student doesn't understand.

Role-play #2
You are riding on a bus. Student B gets on and asks you something.

Role-play #3
You are trying to enjoy a quiet evening in your apartment. Student B is your neighbor, and he or she has the music turned up very loud. Ask your neighbor to turn it down.

Unit 22 The art of crime

3 Read the crime story. Complete the sentences to make your own article. Use your imagination to make the article interesting.

Last night, **(1)** _____ was broken into, and

(2) _____ was stolen. **(3)** _____ and

(4) _____ were attacked by the thief and another

person. Police suspect that the stolen goods were placed

in a **(5)** _____ and taken to **(6)** _____.

Some observers think the crime was an inside job.

4 🎧 Listen to the model conversation.

5 *PAIRS.* Ask questions to find out what your partner's crime story is. Then answer his or her questions about your story.

Unit 23 A balanced life

6 🎧 Listen to the model conversation.

7 *PAIRS.* Ask and answer questions about each other's work and leisure activities.

8 *GROUPS OF 4.* Tell the other pair about your partner's life.

> *Sylvie has a balanced life. She is really into her job and enjoys going to work every day. She doesn't mind her boss, except when he's in a bad mood . . .*

Unit 24 Digital age

9 Think of five items or occupations and write short definitions for them.
Palm Pilot: thing where you can keep your schedule and all your addresses

10 🎧 Listen to the model conversation.

11 *GROUPS OF 3.* Take turns reading your definitions aloud and guessing the answers. The first person to guess each item gets 1 point.

UNIT 25

Arranged marriages

Vocabulary Wedding party; expressions with *get*
Grammar *It's* + adjective / noun + infinitive to express opinion
Speaking Talking about relationships

Lesson A

Getting started

1 **Look at the photo of the wedding party. Identify the people.**

bride _D_   best man ___   bridesmaids ___

groom ___   groomsmen ___   maid of honor ___

2 **Complete the story with the expressions in the boxes.**

got engaged	get on each other's nerves	got to know

1. Carla and Greg _got engaged_ three years ago. During that time, they _____ each other very well! Carla and Greg _____ at times, but most of the time they have a great time together.

get along	got married	gotten over

2. Carla and Greg _____ yesterday. The wedding ceremony was fine, but there was some tension during the reception. Phil, the best man, is Greg's best friend. Jenny, Carla's sister, was the maid of honor. Jenny and Phil went out together for a year. Jenny has never _____ Phil, and she doesn't _____ with Phil's new girlfriend.

get back with	get divorced	got upset

3. At some point during the reception, Jenny told Carla that she would like to _____ Phil. Phil's new girlfriend overheard the conversation and _____. Carla and Greg started arguing about Jenny. People thought they were going to _____ before their honeymoon. After a few minutes, everyone calmed down. Phil told Greg that he was very sorry about the situation.

3 *PAIRS.* **Compare your answers.**

4 *GROUPS OF 3.* **Tell each other about a wedding you've been to recently.**

116

Pronunciation

5 🎧 **Listen. Notice the different pronunciations of _t_ at the end of a word when it links to another _t_ and when it links two vowel sounds.**

went out together   They went out together for three years.

during that time   During that time, they got to know each other well.

get upset   At times, they get upset with each other.

get on each other's nerves   Sometimes they get on each other's nerves.

get along well   But most of the time, they get along well.

6 🎧 **Listen again and repeat.**

Listening

7 *PAIRS.* **What is an arranged marriage? Are they now or were they once common in your country?**

8 🎧 **Listen to Monica and Carlos talk about the movie _Monsoon Wedding._ What does Carlos think of arranged marriages?**

9 🎧 **Listen again. Write _T_ (true) or _F_ (false) after each statement.**

1. In the movie, Aditi's parents want her to marry a man who works in Texas.

2. It's not important for Aditi to marry someone her parents like.

3. Monica thinks that Carlos and his fiancée should see the movie.

4. Carlos will probably go to see _Monsoon Wedding_ with his fiancée.

Grammar focus

1 **Study the examples. Notice the ways to express an opinion.**

> It's **important to know** the person you're marrying.
> It's **important for her to marry someone** her parents like.
> It's **a good idea to let** your parents arrange things.
> It's not **a good idea for her to marry** a stranger.

2 **Look at the examples again. Underline the correct information to complete the rules in the chart.**

It's + adjective/noun to express opinion
It's can be followed by an adjective or a noun **+ infinitive / gerund.**
Use *for* + **subject / object** before the infinitive when you want to specify *who*.

Grammar Reference page 148

3 **Use the words in columns 1 and 3 to write eight logical sentences. Begin each sentence with *It's*. Make some sentences with the words in column 2 to specify *who*.**

It's a bad idea for someone to get married just to please his or her parents.

1	2	3
		get married just to please his or her parents
(not) important		be engaged for three years before getting married
(not) a good idea	someone	get married without getting engaged first
(not) a bad idea	couples	get to know each other well before getting married
(not) crazy	parents	choose children's marriage partners
(not) absurd	people	try to get along with each other's parents
(not) wonderful		marry someone with similar interests
		maintain some independence

4 *PAIRS.* **Compare your sentences.**

Speaking

5 *BEFORE YOU SPEAK.* **Read the advice in the guide and add two more statements.**

The Complete Guide for Couples

♥ You should let your parents help you choose your spouse.

♥ Couples should stay close to their families after getting married.

♥ You should choose someone you have known for a long time.

♥ Both spouses should develop and maintain their own interests.

♥ You should share all your problems with your spouse. Don't keep anything to yourself.

♥ Couples should enjoy doing the same kinds of things.

♥ _____
   _____

♥ _____
   _____

6 *PAIRS.* **Share your opinions about each statement.**

A: *I think it's crazy to let your parents help you choose your spouse.*

B: *Well, I think it's OK to listen to their opinion, but you have to make the final decision, that's for sure.*

7 **Take a class poll. Are there any statements most people agree with?**

Writing

8 **Imagine that you write an advice column for a local newspaper. Today you received this email from a reader. Write your answer. Use *It's* + adjective or noun + infinitive.**

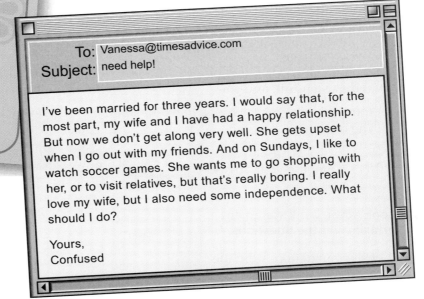

To: Vanessa@timesadvice.com
Subject: need help!

I've been married for three years. I would say that, for the most part, my wife and I have had a happy relationship. But now we don't get along very well. She gets upset when I go out with my friends. And on Sundays, I like to watch soccer games. She wants me to go shopping with her, or to visit relatives, but that's really boring. I really love my wife, but I also need some independence. What should I do?

Yours,
Confused

CONVERSATION TO GO

A: I think it's fine for you to disagree with me all the time.
B: Oh, you're so wrong. I hardly ever argue with you.

UNIT 26 Money matters

Vocabulary Money and banks
Grammar Verbs with two objects
Speaking Talking about money

Getting started

1 Complete the sentences with a pair of expressions in the box. Make the necessary changes.

~~be in the red / be in the black~~	borrow money / lend money
invest money / save money	bank statement / bank account
checking account / savings account	deposit money / withdraw money
receive interest / pay interest	

1. When you owe money, you _are in the red_, but once you pay it all back, you _are in the black_ again.

2. You _____ when you put it in the bank, and you _____ if you need it to buy something.

3. People usually keep money for paying bills in a _____ but put their savings in a _____, so that the bank pays them some interest.

4. Banks usually send their customers a _____ every month explaining the activity in their _____.

5. People _____ on the money they have in the bank, but they _____ on money they borrow from the bank.

6. You _____ when you buy something (or shares in a company) to make a profit, and you _____ when you keep it and don't spend it.

7. You _____ from a bank (or someone) when you need more than you have. The bank (or someone) _____ to you.

2 *PAIRS.* Compare your answers.

3 Look at the bank statement and answer the questions.

1. How much money did the customer deposit?

2. How much money did the customer pay in checks?

3. Did the customer pay or receive interest? How much?

4. Is the customer in the black or in the red?

● **DirBanking**

Statement of account		Checking account number: 81033917		
Date		Credits	Debits	Balance
				2,312.78
08/24	Balance brought forward		17.50	2,295.28
08/29	Check #1075		150.00	2,145.28
09/06	Check #1076	500.00		2,645.28
09/15	Electronic Deposit	14.52		2,659.80
09/21	Interest			2,659.80
09/22	Balance brought forward			

4 *PAIRS.* **Which of the things in Exercise 1 do you do the most?**

Reading

5 *PAIRS.* **Look at the photos showing different ways of banking. Discuss these questions.**

What do you use banks for?

Which of the methods of banking in the pictures do you prefer? Why?

6 **Read the web page for DirBanking. What are three advantages of banking with this online service?**

7 **Read the web page again and answer the questions.**

1. How does DirBanking save you time?

2. Why would you want to borrow money from this bank?

3. How can you access your account?

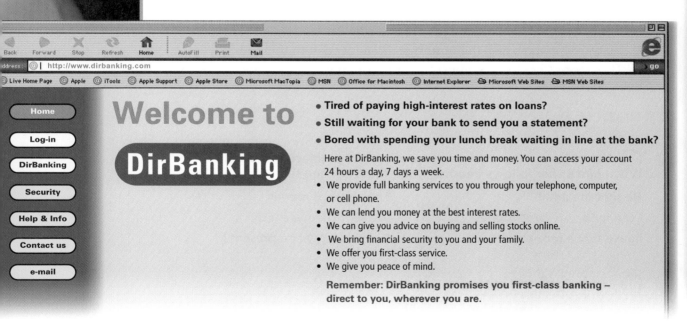

Back Forward Stop Refresh Home AutoFill Print Mail	
Address:	http://www.dirbanking.com	go

Live Home Page   Apple   iTools   Apple Support   Apple Store   Microsoft MacTopia   MSN   Office for Macintosh   Internet Explorer   Microsoft Web Sites   MSN Web Sites

Home

Log-in

DirBanking

Security

Help & Info

Contact us

e-mail

Welcome to

DirBanking

• **Tired of paying high-interest rates on loans?**
• **Still waiting for your bank to send you a statement?**
• **Bored with spending your lunch break waiting in line at the bank?**

Here at DirBanking, we save you time and money. You can access your account 24 hours a day, 7 days a week.
• We provide full banking services to you through your telephone, computer, or cell phone.
• We can lend you money at the best interest rates.
• We can give you advice on buying and selling stocks online.
• We bring financial security to you and your family.
• We offer you first-class service.
• We give you peace of mind.

Remember: DirBanking promises you first-class banking – direct to you, wherever you are.

Grammar focus

1 **Look at the examples with direct and indirect objects. Underline the direct object and circle the indirect object in each sentence.**

> We can lend **you money**.
> We can lend **money to you**.
>
> We bring **your family financial security**.
> We bring **financial security to your family**.

2 **Look at the examples again. Underline the correct words to complete the rules in the chart.**

Verbs with two objects
When the indirect object comes **before** the direct object, **use / do not use** a preposition.
When the indirect object comes **after** the direct object, **use / do not use** a preposition (usually *to* or *for*).

Grammar Reference page 149

3 **Rewrite each sentence by changing the order of the direct and indirect object.**

1. I lent my sister ten dollars.
   I lent ten dollars to my sister.
2. I showed the bank statement to my accountant.
3. Can you send me the bill?
4. She teaches money management to high school students.
5. I can lend the money to you.
6. When will you send me the receipt?
7. Many companies give the option of direct deposit to their employees.
8. The bank offers its customers low-interest loans.

Pronunciation

4 **Listen. Notice the weak pronunciation of the object pronouns. When *him* or *her* follows another word, the h is often silent.**

He sent me a bill.	They owe us money.
I can lend you some money.	We sent them a check.
I gave him a receipt.	Did you buy her a present?

5 **Listen again and repeat.**

6 **Complete the sentences with the word you hear: *her*, *him*, or *them*.**

1. I showed _____ the statement.
2. We owe _____ money.
3. I gave _____ a check.
4. Did you give _____ a receipt?
5. I sent _____ a bill.
6. I lent _____ five dollars.

Speaking

7 *BEFORE YOU SPEAK.*
**Congratulations! You have won
first prize in a contest—$100,000!
Now you have to decide what to
do with the prize money. Make
a list. Be very specific. Use these
ideas or other ideas of your own.**

- buy presents for your friends
  (Who? What presents?)
- keep some for yourself (How much? Invest it?)
- lend some to a friend to start a business (How much? Receive interest?)
- give some to your family (How much?)
- give some to a charity (Which charity? How much?)

8 *GROUPS OF 3.* **Compare your decisions. Ask and answer questions.**

A: *First, I'd buy my younger brother a sports car.*
   That would cost about $40,000.
B: *Wow! That's generous.*
C: *Why would you do that?*

Writing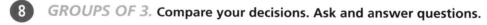

9 **You are the head of an organization that gives money to important social,
community, and educational programs in your city or town. Write a letter
to a rich, local business owner, explaining how you would distribute one
million dollars of his or her money. Use verbs with two objects. Be as
specific as you can.**

CONVERSATION TO GO

A: Can you lend me ten dollars?
B: Sorry, I never lend money to friends!

Lesson A

Less is more

Vocabulary *waste, use, spend, save* + noun
Grammar Review and expansion: *should/shouldn't, could,*
ought to for advice
Speaking Giving advice

Getting started

1 Look at the word web. It shows how the verb *waste* can go with these nouns.

electricity / energy   paper   time

money ——— waste ——— opportunities

space   resources

2 *PAIRS.* Make word webs for the verbs *use, spend,* and *save.* Use the same nouns as in Exercise 1.

Use

Spend

Save

3 🎧 Listen and check your answers.

4 *PAIRS.* Look at the picture of the office. Make as many sentences as possible using the verb + noun combinations from Exercise 1.

A: *They are wasting electricity because all the lights are on.*
B: *And I'm sure they also spend a lot of money on paper.*

124

Listening

5 Underline the words so that the sentences express your opinion.

1. If you want to feel more energetic, then you should sleep **more / less.**
2. If you want to be more effective in business, you should use technology **more / less**.
3. To be more successful at work, work **longer / shorter** hours.
4. Eat **more / less** if you want to be healthier.

6 *PAIRS.* Compare your answers.

7 🎧 Listen to the radio interview with Laura Chang, author of the book *Less Is More*. What does she think about the statements in Exercise 5?

8 🎧 *PAIRS.* Listen again and answer the questions.

1. Why does the author think that people should work shorter hours?

2. What does the author say will happen if a person gets too little sleep? too much sleep?

3. Why does the author say people ought to try taking afternoon naps?

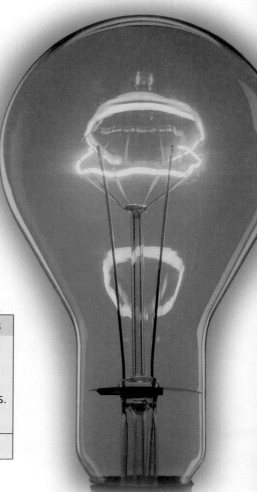

Grammar focus

1 Study the examples with *should*, *could*, and *ought to*.

> **(+)** She's exhausted! She **should work** shorter hours.
> He's so unhealthy. He really **ought to eat** less.
> If they need to use less energy, they could use fluorescent bulbs, or they **could get** solar hot water panels.
>
> **(–)** We **shouldn't sleep** so much on the weekends.
> We never get anything done!
>
> **(?)** I can't finish all my work. What **should** I **do**?

2 Look at the examples again. Complete the rules in the chart with *could*, *should*, or *ought to*.

Modals *could*, *should (not)*, *ought to* for advice and suggestions
Use _____ and *ought to* for advice.
Use _____ for questions.
Use only _____ in questions to ask for advice and suggestions.
Use only _____ in negative for advice.
NOTE: *Ought to* is never used in the negative form.

Grammar Reference page 149

3 Rewrite the sentences using the appropriate form of *should*, *could*, or *ought to*. More than one answer is possible in some cases.

1. I want to have more energy. What is your advice?

   What should I do to have more energy?

2. One day the world will run out of oil, so it's important to invest in solar power now.

3. Don't use incandescent light bulbs. They waste a lot of resources.

4. To have more energy during the day, you have a couple of choices. Either sleep less at night, or take a nap in the afternoon.

5. If you want to save on your electric bill, here's my advice: use fluorescent bulbs as much as possible.

6. They need to get more done at work. What is your advice?

7. Don't leave the lights on if you're not in a room.

8. Here's a suggestion to do better at work: use less technology.

4 *PAIRS.* Compare your answers.

27

Lesson B

Pronunciation

5 🎧 **Listen. Notice the weak pronunciations of** *should* **and** *could* **and the linked pronunciation of** *ought to* **("oughta").**

What should I do?   You should work shorter hours.

You could take an afternoon nap.   You could spend less time at the computer.

You **ought to** relax more.   You **ought to** sleep less.

6 🎧 **Listen again and repeat.**

Speaking

7 *GROUPS OF 3.* **Describe a situation. Ask for and give advice. Student A, look at this page. Student B, look at page 137. Student C, look at page 140.**

Take turns sharing your problems and giving advice on what to do.

Student A

Problem #1
I can read and write English well, but when I try to have a conversation in English, I feel embarrassed. Do you have any suggestions?

Problem #4
It takes me too long to get to work and back home every day. I spend too much time commuting every day. Any ideas?

Problem #7
My colleagues at work always arrive late for meetings. I waste my time waiting for them. Help!

A: Maybe you should try . . .
B: Or, what about this? I think you should . . .

Writing

8 **Think of a problem that a friend or relative has. Write the person a short letter giving him or her advice on that problem. Use the modals** *should/shouldn't, could,* **and** *ought to* **for giving advice.**

CONVERSATION TO GO

A: What should I do?
B: You ought to relax more.

Celebrate

Vocabulary Words related to parties
Grammar Present unreal conditional (*If* + simple past + *would* + verb)
Speaking Talking about imaginary situations

Getting started

1 **Write the words and phrases from the box in the correct columns.**

anniversary	barbecue	birthday	black tie
DJ	dinner	family reunion	graduation
live music	pianist	potluck dinner	wedding

Occasion	Type of party	Music
anniversary	black tie	

2 **Complete the sentences with words from Exercise 1.**

1. The company is having a <u>black tie</u> party, so I guess I'll have to rent a tuxedo.

2. What are you taking to the _____ at Jack's house? I'm taking Thai chicken salad, my specialty!

3. _____ is always better than a DJ, don't you think?

4. I don't have _____ parties because I can't cook.

5. It's such a hot day. Let's have a _____ at the lake.

6. Jan's having a big _____ party in her backyard on Saturday. She's turning twenty-one on Friday.

7. My brother and I gave a party for my parents' twenty-fifth _____. All their friends and our family came.

3 *PAIRS.* **Compare your answers.**

Reading

4 A magazine is holding a competition. Read the advertisement and answer the questions.

1. Why is the magazine having a competition?
2. What do you have to do to enter?
3. What's the prize?

5 *PAIRS.* Match the sentences with the pictures below.

1. If we had a formal dinner with the family, my parents would love it. __B__

2. If it were possible, I would have fireworks. _____

3. I'd have a party on a yacht if money were not a problem. _____

4. If the children couldn't come, it wouldn't be a real family reunion. _____

5. If we had live music, people would have a great time. _____

6. I would not serve the food myself if I had the money to hire a waitress. _____

It's party time

Help us celebrate our

100th edition

Win the party of a lifetime for someone you love. We'll pay for everything.

All you have to do is tell us your party plans. If you had the chance to have the party of a lifetime, who would it be for, when would you have the party, and what would you celebrate?

If money were no problem,

- what type of party would it be?
- where would you have the party?
- what food and drink would you choose?
- how many people would you invite?

To enter the competition you must be 18 or over. The competition closes on December 31.

(A)

(B)

Grammar focus

1 **Study the examples of the present unreal conditional.**

> **(+) If** I **were** a millionaire, I**'d have** a party on a yacht.
> **(–)** It **wouldn't be** a family reunion **if** the children **couldn't come**.
> **(?) If** you **invited** all your friends to a party, where **would** it **be**?

2 **Look at the examples again. Underline the correct information to complete the rules in the chart.**

Present unreal conditional
Use the present unreal conditional to talk about **real / imaginary** situations.
The verb in the *if* clause is in the **base form / past tense**.
Use **would / should** in the result clause.
Use a comma when the *if* clause comes **first / last**.
NOTE: Use *were* for all forms of *be*.

> *Grammar Reference page 149*

3 **Rewrite the sentences using the present unreal conditional.**

1. I live in a small apartment, so I don't have large parties.
   If I didn't have a small apartment, I'd have large parties.
2. I don't have enough money, so I can't take a long vacation.
3. Etsu doesn't like to cook. That's why she invited us to a restaurant.
4. I don't have a barbecue every weekend only because I don't have a backyard.
5. Imad never invites his friends to his house because he lives too far out of town.
6. Magali is not a good dancer. That's why she doesn't go to clubs with her friends.
7. My neighbors complain about the noise, so I can't have a lot of parties.
8. A beach party is a great way to celebrate a birthday, but mine is in the winter.

Pronunciation

4 🎧 **Listen. Notice the pronunciation of the weak and contracted forms of *would*.**

Where **would** it be?   If you could have a party, where **would** it be?

I'd have the party at a restaurant.   I **wouldn't** cook.

We'd have live music.   They'd play salsa.

We'd dance all night.   Everyone **would** have a great time.

5 🎧 **Listen again and repeat.**

Speaking

6 *BEFORE YOU SPEAK.* **What is your idea of a perfect party? Enter the competition. Take notes.**

100th Edition "Party of a Lifetime"
Official Competition Entry Form

Place _____

Time/Occasion _____

Type of party _____

Food and drink _____

Music _____

Number of people _____

(Other ideas) _____

_____

_____

7 *GROUPS OF 3.* **Tell each other about your party and answer questions about it. Then vote for the winning entry.**

My party would be a surprise party for my boyfriend. It would be . . .

8 **Tell the class about your party.**

Writing

9 **Write an invitation to the party you have arranged. Be creative and include information about the points on the list.**

- occasion (reason for the party)
- type of party
- when and where the party is
- how to get there
- dress code (casual, elegant, . . .)

CONVERSATION TO GO

A: What would you do if you won a competition?
B: If I won a lot of money, I'd throw myself a big going-away party at work!

131

Unit 25 Arranged marriages

1 🎧 Listen to the model conversation.

2 *PAIRS.* What do you think makes a successful marriage? Use the phrases in the chart and your own ideas to make five statements expressing your opinion.

I think it's . . .	a good idea . . .	(for . . .) to . . .
	a bad idea . . .	get married
	crazy / absurd / wonderful . . .	get to know each other
	very / somewhat / not very important . . .	get engaged
		get upset
		get along
		get over something

Unit 26 Money matters

3 🎧 Listen to the model conversation.

4 *GROUPS OF 4.* Student A, you have just won a million dollars and you're trying to keep it a secret. Students B, C, and D, you've heard about Student A's winnings and are visiting him or her. Read your situation and then have a conversation. Keep talking until you reach an agreement.

Student A's situation: You're planning to have a family someday. You need this money to provide you and your family with financial security.

Student B's situation: You loaned Student A some money back in high school but he or she never paid you back. Now you want him or her to pay back what he or she owes—with interest!

Student C's situation: You have a great idea for a new business, but the bank won't give you a loan. You want Student A to invest some money in the business. He or she would be your partner.

Student D's situation: You were best friends with Student A when you were children. Now you are the president of a charity that helps feed hungry people all over the world. You want Student A to donate some of his or her money to this charity.

Unit 27 Less is more

5 🎧 Listen to the model conversation.

6 *PAIRS.* Role-play. You have one of the problems below. Use your imagination to add details. Take turns asking for and giving advice.

You . . .
  spend too much time working/sleeping/shopping . . .
  don't spend enough time with your family/at your work/with your friends . . .
  don't have enough space to work/exercise/cook . . .
  spend too much money on clothes/food/jewelry . . .
  waste too much time on the Internet/playing cards/watching TV . . .

Unit 28 Celebrate

7 🎧 Listen to the model conversation and look at the pictures.

8 *GROUPS OF 3.* Take turns asking and answering *what if* . . . questions about the situations below. Give reasons for your answers. Who has the most original idea?

• win a contest
• don't have to go to school or work every day
• don't need to worry about money
• can live anywhere in the world
• have all the free time you want
• have dinner with a famous person

World of Music 4

Vocabulary

1 *GROUPS OF 3.* **What do you think these sentences mean? Choose the best answer.**

1. I'd take back those words that hurt you.
   a. I'd return that book to the store if you don't like it.
   b. I wish I hadn't said those hurtful things to you.
   c. I wish I hadn't done those terrible things to you.
2. Pride's like a knife; it can cut deep inside.
   a. Sharp knives are dangerous.
   b. Pride is similar to a knife because they can both cut you.
   c. Pride is similar to a knife because they can both hurt people.
3. Words are like weapons; they wound sometimes.
   a. Words can hurt someone as badly as a weapon.
   b. People can injure others easily if they aren't careful.
   c. People need to be careful with weapons because they might wound someone.

Listening

2 🎧 **Listen to the song. Which word best describes the feelings of the speaker?**

a. regretful   b. worried   c. joyful

*Known for her outrageous costumes and wigs, **Cher** has faded from popularity many times over her long career but has always managed to emerge again into the limelight. If I Could Turn Back Time is one of Cher's many "comeback" songs.*

3 🎧 **Listen to the song and put each line of the chorus in order.**

4 *PAIRS.* **Compare your answers.**

Speaking

5 *GROUPS OF 3.* **Discuss the questions. Explain your opinions and ask and answer follow-up questions.**

1. What do you think the story behind this song might be?
2. What might have happened to make the singer feel the way she does?

If I Could Turn Back Time

If I could turn back time

If I could find a way

I'd take back those words that have hurt you and you'd stay

I don't know why I did the things I did

I don't know why I said the things I said

Pride's like a knife it can cut deep inside

Words are like weapons, they wound sometimes

I didn't really mean to hurt you

I didn't wanna see you go

I know I made you cry, but baby

CHORUS

back / time / if / could / turn / I _____

way / if / could / I / find / a _____

take / I'd / back / words / those / you / hurt / that _____

you'd / and / stay _____

I / the / reach / if / could/ stars _____

you / to / give / all / I'd / them _____

then you'd love me, love me,

used / do / to / you / like _____

I / time / back / if / could / turn _____

My world was shattered I was torn apart

Like someone took a knife and drove it

deep in my heart

You walked out that door I swore that I didn't care

but I lost everything darling then and there

Too strong to tell you I was sorry

CHORUS

Unit 1, Exercise 6
Student A

Student A, this is your situation. Complete each sentence with information that is true for you. Use your imagination and add at least two more details!

- You went to high school (secondary school) with Student B, but you haven't seen each other in a few years.
- You used to be an actor, but now you're working at _____.
- You're taking _____ classes.
- You're living in _____.
- _____
- _____
- Ask about Student B's job and what he or she is doing these days.
- End your conversation.

Unit 7, Exercise 4
Student B

Student B, your impressions of the restaurant include:

- atmosphere not formal enough—hard to have a conversation
- waiters couldn't answer questions, not knowledgeable enough about the menu items
- pizzas were too bland and fatty—not enough spices and too much cheese
- good salad, but dressing too sweet
- only offered soft drinks—no iced tea or hot beverages
- much too expensive

With your partner, decide if you would go back to that restaurant again.

A: *I thought the salad was really fresh.*
B: *Yes, but I didn't like the dressing. I thought it was too sweet.*
A: *Really? I didn't think it was sweet enough. It seemed sour to me.*

Unit 3, Exercise 4
Student B

Read the brochure. Then take turns asking and answering questions about the facilities and services at your partner's hotel. Both hotels cost $115 per night. Together, choose one of the hotels.

A: *How many rooms does the Delta Hotel have?*
B: *It has 32 rooms. Does the Marina offer free airport transportation?*

The Delta Hotel

A cozy, charming hotel located in the heart of downtown offering:

- free airport transportation
- 32 guest rooms, each decorated with antique furniture and paintings
- television and telephone in all rooms, with high-speed Internet access
- exercise room and sauna
- 24-hour coffee shop and café

Our concierge will be happy to assist you with theater or opera tickets and can recommend fine restaurants within walking distance of the hotel.

Review 6, Exercise 2
Student B

Role-play #1

Student A is your teacher. He or she is explaining a math problem, but you don't understand. Ask the teacher to explain it again.

Role-play #2

You get on a bus with your elderly grandmother. Student A is sitting in the seat near the door. You ask him or her to let your grandmother sit there.

Role-play #3

You are having a party with some friends. Student A is your neighbor. He or she comes to your door to ask you something.

Unit 4, Exercise 7
Student A

You're a patient. Don't give the doctor your information all at once. Try to make the doctor ask you questions to find out what your problem might be. Choose one of the following situations:

- **Situation 1:** You have the following symptoms: red eyes, itchy throat, runny nose, headache. You arrive at the doctor's office very tired and depressed.

- **Situation 2:** You have the following symptoms: You have a very bad rash on your hands and face. It's red and itchy and painful. You have had it for almost a week. You never drink coffee or tea or milk. You only eat chocolate on special occasions. You don't have any pets, but you did go horseback riding last weekend. You went to the zoo two weeks ago.

- **Situation 3:** Your choice. You choose the symptoms.

Unit 27, Exercise 7
Student B

Take turns sharing your problems and giving advice on what to do.

A: Maybe you should try . . .
B: Or, what about this? I think you should . . .

Problem #2

I have a computer at home, but I can't use it much because every time I try to download something, it tells me it's out of memory. What can I do?

Problem #5

I have no problem learning new English words in class, but after a day or two, I always forget the new words or what they mean. What would you suggest?

Problem #8

I feel that I'm not saving enough money. I want to spend less and save more, but how?

Unit 9, Exercise 6
Student A

You and Student B are taking a weekend trip to Washington, D.C., together. Ask Student B questions and fill in the missing itinerary information about your trip. Remember to use the simple present to ask for information about schedules, timetables, and events. Answer Student B's questions.

A: What airline are we on?
B: We're on . . .

WorldView Travel

Here is your itinerary. Have a great trip!

FLIGHT INFORMATION

Airline: <u>Jet Airways</u>   Ticket/class: _____

to Washington, D.C.   **from Washington, D.C.**

Day/date: Friday, April 19   Day/date: Sunday, April 21
Time departs: _____   Time departs: _____
Time arrives: _____   Time arrives: _____

HOTEL INFORMATION

The Wellington Hotel
(Located 5 blocks from the White House)

Arrival date: Friday, April 19   Check-in time: 1:00 P.M.
Departure date: Sunday, April 21   Check-out time: 11:00 A.M.
Free airport transfers

Unit 17, Exercise 5

3–4 *a* answers: You have very little willpower and find it difficult to control your mind and body. Try harder!

3–4 *b* answers: It is easy for you to achieve things by controlling your mind and body. You have a lot of willpower. Congratulations!

3–4 *c* answers: You are like most people . . . you have some willpower, but not enough. Don't give up!

Unit 1, Exercise 6
Student B

Student B, this is your situation. Complete each sentence with information that is true for you. Use your imagination and add at least two more details!

- You went to high school (secondary school) with Student A, but you haven't seen each other in a few years.
- You're a/an (your occupation). You're working at _____ .
- You're also taking _____ classes.
- _____
- _____
- Ask Student A where he or she is living now.
- Ask Student A if he or she is still acting.
- End your conversation.

Review 1, Exercise 8
Student B

Student B, use this information to answer Student A's questions.

Super Seven Hotel
- a budget motel with all the comforts of home
- just minutes from the airport
- 78 rooms ($59/night), all with television and telephone
- 24-hour coffee shop and café
- exercise room and sauna
- a conference room
- computer hookups and fax service available
- free baby-sitting service 24 hours a day

Unit 24, Exercise 4
Student A

Look at the cues and follow the model to make unfinished sentences using who, that/which, and where. Do not say the answer (in parentheses). Take turns saying your unfinished sentences to your group. The person who finishes it first with the correct answer gets 1 point.

A: A person who flies planes is . . .
B: A pilot.
A: Correct. You get a point.

1. person / flies planes
   (a pilot)
   A person who flies planes is . . .
2. machine / cooks food very fast
   (a microwave oven)
3. place / people store their books
   (a bookshelf)
4. movie / very scary
   (a horror movie)
5. man / getting married
   (a groom)
6. place / you can rent a room for a night
   (a hotel)

Unit 13, Exercise 8
Students A and B

You are a married couple in the U.S. Student A is from the U.S. Student B is from another country. Immigration officers are going to interview you both, but separately. You have five minutes to prepare for the interview. Work together to make sure you give the same information about:

- how long Student B has been in the U.S.
- how long you have known each other/been married
- where you met
- what your favorite thing about the other person is
- your wedding
- your jobs
- what you do in your free time

When the teacher calls "Time," go to page 63, Exercise 9.

Unit 8, Exercise 6
Student A

You are a very neat and responsible person. You enjoy cooking, you study a lot, and you always get to bed before 10:00 P.M. You wake up at 6:00 A.M. You love classical music.

These are some of the things you want your roommate to agree to. He or she has to:
• keep the house neat and clean
• take out the trash every day
• do his or her own laundry at least once a week
• take turns doing the housework
• pay 50% of all the bills

He or she can't:
• play loud music after 10:00 P.M.
• be late in paying the bills

Work out an agreement with your partner. Take notes on page 37.

You don't have to go to bed early, but you have to be quiet if you're up after ten, so you can't play loud music then.

Review 4, Exercise 2
Students A and B

1. **Students A and B, you are roommates. Prepare for a meeting with your new landlord.**

   Decide how long you've:
   lived in the U.S. _____
   known each other _____
   shared an apartment _____
   taken English classes together _____

2. **Ask these questions to find out whether or not Students C and D are really roommates.**

   How long have you:
   lived in the U.S.? _____
   known each other? _____
   shared an apartment? _____
   taken English classes together? _____
   had your dog? _____

Unit 9, Exercise 6
Student B

You and Student A are taking a weekend trip to Washington, D.C., together. Ask Student A questions and fill in the missing itinerary information about your trip. Remember to use the simple present to ask for information about schedules, timetables, and events. Answer Student A's questions.

A: What airline are we on?
B: We're on . . .

WorldView Travel

Here is your itinerary. Have a great trip!

FLIGHT INFORMATION

Airline: Jet Airways

to Washington, D.C.

Ticket/class: business class

from Washington, D.C.

Day/date: _____
Time departs: 7:00 A.M.
Time arrives: 12:00 noon

Day/date: _____
Time departs: 4:00 P.M.
Time arrives: 9:00 P.M.

HOTEL INFORMATION

The Wellington Hotel
(Located _____)
Arrival date: _____
Departure date: _____
Free airport transfers

Check-in time: _____
Check-out time: _____

139

Unit 13, Exercise 8
Students C and D

You are immigration officers in the U.S. Students A and B are married. Student A is from the U.S. Student B is from another country. You think they may not have a real marriage. You have five minutes to work together to prepare questions to ask the couple. You will ask Students A and B the same questions separately and then compare their answers. Write your questions on a piece of paper. Ask questions about:

• how long Student B has been in the country
• how long they have known each other/been married
• where they met
• what their favorite thing about the other person is
• their wedding (When? Where? How many people attended? How long it lasted?)
• their jobs
• what they do in their free time

When the Teacher calls "Time," go to page 63, Exercise 9.

Review 4, Exercise 2
Students C and D

1. Ask these questions to find out whether or not Students A and B are really roommates.

   How long have you:
   lived in the U.S.? _____
   known each other? _____
   shared an apartment? _____
   taken English classes together? _____
   worked at the same place? _____

2. Students C and D, you are roommates. Prepare for a meeting with your new landlord.

   Decide how long you've:
   lived in the U.S. _____
   known each other _____
   shared an apartment _____
   taken English classes together _____

Unit 22, Exercise 8
Student A

1. Read the text and ask Student B questions to find out the missing information.

A: What was stolen from a train?

In England in 1963, (1) _____ was stolen from a train. The crime was called (2) _____. The train was stopped near (3) _____. The driver was attacked, and the train was then driven one kilometer down the track. One hundred and twenty bags of bills were stolen. The money was taken (4) _____, where the robbers even used some of it to play Monopoly. But very soon, the thirteen main thieves were arrested, and most of the money was recovered.

2. Now answer Student B's questions.

Unit 27, Exercise 7
Student C

Take turns sharing your problems and giving advice on what to do.

A: Maybe you should try . . .
B: Or, what about this? I think you should . . .

Problem #3

I'm out of shape and need to do more exercise. But running seems a waste of energy. Any ideas?

Problem #6

I never remember my friends' birthdays. OK, it saves money on cards and presents. But what's the answer?

Problem #9

I like everyone in class, but I feel more comfortable working alone than with others. Do you have any suggestions?

Unit 24, Exercise 4
Student B

Look at the cues and follow the model to make unfinished sentences using *who*, *that/which*, and *where*. Do not say the answer (in parentheses). Take turns saying your unfinished sentences to your group. The person who finishes it first with the correct answer gets 1 point.

B: A person who writes with his or her left hand is . . .
C: A lefty.
B: Correct.

1. person / writes with his or her left hand
   (a lefty)
2. plastic thing / you use instead of money
   (a credit card)
3. place / you can see famous paintings
   (a museum)
4. movie / makes you laugh
   (a comedy)
5. place in a hotel / you check in
   (a lobby)
6. woman / getting married
   (a bride)

Review 1, Exercise 8
Student A

Student A, use this information to answer Student B's questions.

The Drake Hotel
- a classic hotel in the heart of the city
- 5 minutes from fabulous stores, restaurants, and museums
- free transportation to and from the airport
- 153 modern rooms ($219/night) and 25 guest suites ($359/night)
- satellite TV, computer and fax hook-ups in all rooms
- a large ballroom
- 2 conference rooms
- 24-hour business service and translation service
- a fitness center
- an award-winning restaurant and café

Unit 8, Exercise 6
Student B

You are not a very neat person. You have no idea how to cook. You always go out to restaurants, and you like to have fun. Often you don't come home until after midnight. You love rock and roll music and like to play it loud on your stereo.

These are some of the things you want your roommate to agree to. He or she has to:
- do the housework
- not make a fuss if your room is messy
- let you invite friends over for parties
- keep his or her CDs and tapes separate from yours
- let you play rock and roll anytime
- not worry if the bills don't get paid on time

He or she can't:
- make noise before noon
- expect you to be home for dinner

Work out an agreement with your partner. Take notes on page 37.

I'm usually out late, so you can't make noise before noon. You don't have to leave the house, you just have to be quiet.

Unit 22, Exercise 8
Student B

1. Read the text and answer Student A's questions.

In England, in 1963, almost four million dollars was stolen from a train. The crime was called the Great Train Robbery. The train was stopped near London. **(1)** _____ was attacked, and the train was then driven one kilometer down the track. **(2)** _____ bags of bills were stolen. The money was taken to a farm, where the robbers even used some of it to play Monopoly. But very soon, **(3)** _____ were arrested, and **(4)** _____ was recovered.

2. Now ask Student A questions to find out the missing information in your text.

Unit 24, Exercise 4
Student C

Look at the cues and follow the model to make unfinished sentences using *who, that/which,* and *where.* Do not say the answer (in parentheses). Take turns saying your unfinished sentence to your group. The person who finishes it first with the correct answer gets 1 point.

C: A movie that has lots of fights and explosions is . . .
B: A thriller.
C: No.
A: An action movie.
C: Correct. You get a point.

1. movie / has lots of fights and explosions
   (an action movie)
2. person / decorate homes or offices
   (an interior designer)
3. place / you go to work out
   (a fitness center)
4. person / tricks people into giving him or her money
   (a con artist)

5. TV program / usually involves love
   (a soap opera)
6. place / doctors and nurses work
   (a hospital)

Unit 21, Exercise 7
Student B

Role-play #1

Student A is your close friend. Listen and reply.

Role-play #2

You're in a new office and don't know where the light switches are. Ask a co-worker, Student A, to turn on the lights.

Role-play #3

Student A is your employee. Listen and reply.

Role-play #4

Your friends are visiting and want to listen to music. Ask your neighbor, Student A, if you can turn the volume up.

Role-play #5

Student A is your friend. Listen and reply.

Grammar reference

Unit 15

Will/won't for future

- Use **will** and **won't** to talk about the future.
  *Sanjay and Nina **will** get married.*
  *Nina's parents **won't** be happy.*

- Use **think** and **don't think** followed by a subject +
  will to express opinions about future events.
  *I **think** Nina **will** convince her parents.*
  *I **don't think** they **will** cause any problems.*
  *Nina **thinks** they will have children someday.*
  *She **doesn't think** they'll live in London forever.*

Unit 16

Future real conditional (*If* + simple present + *will*)

- Use two clauses to make future real conditional
  statements.

If clause	Result clause
if + simple present	*will/won't* + base form of the verb

- Use the future real conditional to talk about things
  that may happen in the future and their results.
  *If you **eat** this cereal, you'**ll** be strong and healthy.*
  *If you **don't hurry**, we'**ll** be late.*
  *If I **call** you tonight, **will you** be home?*

- The *if* clause is often in the first position in a
  sentence, but it can also go second.
  *He'**ll** fix the washing machine **if** it **breaks**.*

Grammar reference

Unit 17

Verbs + gerund and verbs + infinitive

- Use an infinitive after these verbs: **decide, learn, need, promise, want.**
  I want to go out tonight.
  José doesn't need to buy any new clothes.
  Have you decided to start a diet?

- Use a gerund after these verbs: **cut down on, dislike, enjoy, get out of, give up, keep on, practice, quit, stop, take up.**
  We gave up eating meat.
  I don't enjoy cooking.
  Is Karen taking up swimming?

Notes:
- Gerund = base form of the verb + **–ing**
- Infinitive = **to** + base form of the verb

Unit 18

Used to and would

- Use **used to/would** + base form of the verb to talk about repeated actions in the past that don't happen now.
  A lot of people used to waste energy (but now they don't).
  They didn't use to recycle most materials.
  Did you use to buy cars that used a lot of gas?
  I'd use things once and throw them away.
  We wouldn't turn down the heat at night.

- Use **used to** + base form of the verb to talk about states in the past that aren't that way now.
  Energy sources used to seem endless.
  People didn't use to know that they were hurting the environment.
  Did she use to think that recycling was important?

Unit 19

Passive (simple present)

- Use the passive when:
  - you're not interested in who or what does the action.
  - it's not important who or what does the action.
  - you don't know who or what does the action.

- The object of an active sentence becomes the subject of a passive sentence.
  People make the boxes.   (active)
  The boxes are made.   (passive)

Simple present passive
subject + **am/is/are** + past participle
The boxes are made in Morocco.
They are sold for $75.
The wood is cut by hand.
How are the boxes made? They are made by hand.

Unit 20

So, too, either, neither

- Use **so** and **too** to make additions to affirmative statements.
  He was surprised by the ending, and I was, too.
  He was surprised by the ending, and so was I.

- Use **not** + **either** and **neither** to make additions to negative statements.
  The acting wasn't great, and the story wasn't either.
  The acting wasn't great, and neither was the story.

- Place the auxiliary, modal, or form of **be** or **do** before the subject in an addition with **so** or **neither**.

- Always use an auxiliary, a modal, or a form of **be** or **do** to make an addition. In the addition, use the appropriate form of the same auxiliary, modal, **be**, or **do** that appears in the statement.
  Renée Zellweger starred in the movie Chicago, *and so did Catherine Zeta-Jones.*
  She is a big fan of Keanu Reeves, and I am, too.
  Star Wars *didn't make as much money as* Titanic, *and* E.T. *didn't either.*
  Ben Affleck wasn't in The Lord of the Rings, *and neither was Leonardo DiCaprio.*

Unit 21

Modals: *could you, would you, would you mind . . . ?* for polite requests

- Use **could you** and **would you** followed by the base form of the verb to make polite requests.

Could you	open the window?	Of course.
	please turn off the lights?	
	make less noise?	
Would you	turn up the volume?	Sure.
	stop doing that, please?	

- You can also use **would you mind** followed by a gerund to make polite requests.

Would you mind	closing the door?	No, of course not.
	please turn on the lights?	
	speaking louder?	
	turning down the volume?	
	continuing that, please?	Not at all.

Unit 22

Passive (simple past)

- Use the simple past passive when the action is more important than the person or thing that did the action.

Simple past passive
Subject + **was/were** + past participle
*The cars **were stolen** on Tuesday.*
*A window **was broken.***

- The object of an active sentence becomes the subject of the passive sentence.
*Someone found **my wallet.***
***My wallet** was found.*

- Use **by** + the person or thing to say who or what did the action.
*The manager **was hurt by** the robber.*
*The building **wasn't hit by** lightning.*
*What **was** the car **hit by**?*

Unit 23

Review: verbs for likes/dislikes followed by gerunds and/or infinitives

- Use a gerund or an infinitive after these verbs: **like**, **hate**, **love**, and **can('t) stand**.
*I **like to go** to the gym, but I **hate to lift** weights.*
*She **likes doing** aerobics, but she **hates running**.*
*We **love to eat** fatty foods, but we **can't stand to gain weight**!*
*They **love exercising** outside, but they **hate getting** a sunburn.*

- Use only a gerund after these verbs and phrasal verbs: **mind**, **enjoy**, **be sick of**, and **be into**.
*I don't **mind walking**; it's good exercise!*
*Do you **enjoy working** out?*
*He was **sick of taking** the same kinds of classes at the gym, and now he**'s into doing** Pilates.*

Unit 24

Relative clauses with *that, which, who,* and *where*

- Use relative clauses with **that**, **which**, **who**, and **where** to define people, places, and things.
*A producer is someone **who** makes TV programs.*
*This is the computer **which** we saw at the first store.*
*A cell phone is something **that** makes communication convenient.*
*A garage is a place **where** you can park a car.*

- Use **who** or **that** for people, **which** or **that** for things, and **where** for places.

Unit 25

It's + adjective/noun + infinitive to express opinion

- Use **It's** followed by an adjective or a noun phrase and an infinitive to express an opinion. You can add **for** + an object after the adjective or noun phrase, but it's not necessary.

It's	absurd	(**for** + people) to get married.
	crazy	
	important	
	wonderful	
	a good idea	
	a bad idea	

*It's a good idea **to discuss** issues before marriage.*
*It's a good idea **for couples to discuss** issues before marriage.*
*It's important **to compromise** in a marriage.*
*It's important **for people to compromise** in a marriage.*

Unit 26

Verbs with two objects

• Some verbs can have a direct object. A direct object receives the action of the verb. A direct object answers the question **what** or **who**.
*I received **my bank statement**.* (What did I receive? My bank statement.)
*The accountant didn't return **her call**.* (What didn't he return? The call.)
*When did you see **her**?* (Who did you see? Her.)

• Some verbs can also have an indirect object. An indirect object can come before the direct object. It answers the question *to whom* or *for whom*. The indirect object is usually a person.
*We offer **customers** first-class service.* (Who do we offer service to? Customers.)
*He doesn't owe **the accountant** money.* (Who doesn't he owe the money to? The accountant.)
*Did the bank send **you** a letter?* (Who was the letter for? You.)

• Use **to** or **for** + the indirect object when it follows the direct object.
*We offer first-class service **to customers**.*
*He doesn't owe money **to the accountant**.*
*Did the bank send a letter **to you**?*

Note: You can never have an indirect object without a direct object.
✗ I gave my accountant.

Unit 27

Review: Modals: *should/shouldn't, could, ought to* for advice

• Use **should, could,** or **ought to** tell someone you think something is a good idea.
*You **should** get more sleep.*
*We **could** try going to bed earlier.*
*They **ought to** do more exercise during the day.*

• Use **should** to ask for advice.
*What **should** I do?*
*What time **should** we leave?*

• Use **shouldn't** to tell someone you think something is a bad idea.
*You **shouldn't** work so hard.*
*We **shouldn't** wait too long.*

Unit 28

Present unreal conditional (*If* + simple past + *would* + verb)

• Use two clauses to make present unreal conditional statements.

If clause	Result clause
if + simple past	*would/wouldn't* + base form of the verb

• Use the present unreal conditional to talk about unreal events or conditions in the present and their results.
***If** I **had** a million dollars, I'**d** throw a huge party.*
***If** her hip **didn't hurt**, Grandma **would** dance.*
***If** it **weren't** so far away, we'**d** all go to your house.*
***Would** you come to the party **if** you **had** time?*

• The **if** clause is often in the first position in a sentence, but it can also go second.
*It **wouldn't** be difficult **if** everyone **helped** out.*

Note: Always use the **were** form of the verb **be** in the **if** clause with the present unreal conditional.
*If I **were** you . . .*
*If she **were** nicer . . .*
*If they **weren't** so tired . . .*

Irregular Verbs

Simple present	Simple past	Past Participle	Simple present	Simple past	Past Participle
be	was/were	been	lose	lost	lost
become	became	become	make	made	made
begin	began	begun	mean	meant	meant
break	broke	broken	meet	met	met
build	built	built	pay	paid	paid
buy	bought	bought	put	put	put
catch	caught	caught	quit	quit	quit
choose	chose	chose	ride	rode	ridden
come	came	come	read	read	read
cost	cost	cost	run	ran	run
do	did	done	say	said	said
draw	drew	drawn	see	saw	seen
drink	drank	drunk	sell	sold	sold
drive	drove	driven	send	sent	sent
eat	ate	eaten	shake	shook	shaken
fall	fell	fallen	show	showed	shown
feel	felt	felt	sing	sang	sung
fight	fought	fought	sit	sat	sat
find	found	found	sleep	slept	slept
fly	flew	flown	speak	spoke	spoken
forget	forgot	forgotten	spend	spent	spent
get	got	gotten	stand	stood	stood
give	gave	given	swim	swam	swum
go	went	gone	take	took	taken
grow	grew	grown	teach	taught	taught
hang	hung	hung	tell	told	told
have	had	had	think	thought	thought
hear	heard	heard	throw	threw	thrown
hurt	hurt	hurt	understand	understood	understood
keep	kept	kept	wear	wore	worn
know	knew	known	win	won	won
leave	left	left	write	wrote	written
lend	lent	lent			

Vocabulary

Unit 14
cheer
clap
cry
laugh
scream
shout
whistle
yawn

Unit 15
crime
death
family life
greed
illness
marriage
misfortune
money
power
romance

Unit 16
clean
delicious
fast
fresh
healthy
reliable
safe
shiny
soft

Unit 17
cut back on
cut down on
get out of
give up
keep on
take up
throw away
turn down

Unit 18
alternative medicine
genetic engineering
hybrid cars
instant messaging
renewable resources
telecommuting
vegetarianism

Unit 19
cotton
glass
gold
leather
pewter
lycra
silver
wood

accessories
bathing suit
bicycling shorts
box
candlesticks
clothes/clothing
dress
earrings
gloves
jewelry
mirror
picture frame
ring
sandals
shirt
tray
vase
watch

Unit 20
action movie
animated film
comedy
drama
horror movie
martial arts film
musical
science fiction movie
thriller
western

Unit 21
go off
switch off
switch over to
turn down
turn off
turn on
turn up

Unit 22
robbery/robber/rob
burglary/burglar/burglarize
mugging/mugger/mug
scam/con artist/scam
shoplifting/shoplifter/shoplift
theft/thief/steal

get arrested
go to prison
pay a fine
do community service

Unit 23

take a break
take it easy
take off
take on
take part in
take up

Unit 24

cell phone
computer
digital camera
digital TV
DVD player
laptop
printer
scanner

Unit 25

best man
bride
bridesmaids
ceremony
groom
groomsmen
honeymoon
maid of honor
reception

get along
get back with
get divorced
get engaged
get married
get on each other's nerves
get over
get to know
get upset

Unit 26

bank account
bank statement
be in the black/red
borrow money
checking account
deposit money
invest money
lend money
pay interest
receive interest
save money
savings account
withdraw money

Unit 27

save energy
save money
save paper
save resources
save space
save time
spend money
spend time
use electricity
use money
use paper
use resources
use space
use time
waste electricity/energy
waste money
waste opportunities
waste paper
waste resources
waste space
waste time

Unit 28

anniversary
barbecue
birthday
black tie
DJ
dinner
family reunion
graduation
live music
pianist
potluck dinner
wedding

Acknowledgments

The authors and series editor wish to acknowledge with gratitude the following reviewers, consultants, and piloters for their thoughtful contributions to the development of *WorldView*.

BRAZIL: São Paulo: Sérgio Gabriel, **FMU/Cultura Inglesa, Jundiaí;** Heloísa Helena Medeiros Ramos, **Kiddy and Teen;** Zaina Nunes, Márcia Mathias Pinto, Angelita Goulvea Quevedo, **Pontifícia Universidade Católica;** Rosa Laquimia Souza, **FMU-FIAM;** Élcio Camilo Alves de Souza, Marie Adele Ryan, **Associação Alumni;** Maria Antonieta Gagliardi, **Centro Britânico;** Chris Ritchie, Debora Schisler, Sandra Natalini, **Sevenidiomas;** Joacyr Oliveira, **FMU;** Maria Thereza Garrelhas Gentil, **Colégio Mackenzie;** Carlos Renato Lopes, **Uni-Santana;** Yara M. Bannwart Rago, **Associação Escola Graduada de São Paulo;** Jacqueline Zilberman, **Instituto King's Cross;** Vera Lúcia Cardoso Berk, **Talkative Idioms Center;** Ana Paula Hoepers, **Instituto Winners;** Carlos C.S. de Celis, Daniel Martins Neto, **CEL-LEP;** Maria Carmen Castellani, **União Cultural Brasil Estados Unidos;** Kátia Martins P. de Moraes Leme, **Colégio Pueri Domus;** Luciene Martins Farias, **Aliança Brasil Estados Unidos;** Neide Aparecida Silva, **Cultura Inglesa;** Áurea Shinto, **Santos:** Maria Lúcia Bastos, **Instituto Four Seasons. COLOMBIA: Bogota:** Sergio Monguí, Rafael Díaz Morales, **Universidad de la Salle;** Yecid Ortega Páez, Yojanna Ruiz G., **Universidad Javeriana;** Merry García Metzger, **Universidad Minuto de Dios;** Maria Caterina Barbosa, **Coninglés;** Nelson Martínez R., **Asesorías Académicas;** Eduardo Martínez, Stella Lozano Vega, **Universidad Santo Tomás de Aquino;** Kenneth McIntyre, **ABC English Institute. JAPAN: Tokyo:** Peter Bellars, **Obirin University;** Michael Kenning, **Takushoku University;** Martin Meldrum, **Takushoku University;** Carol Ann Moritz, **New International School;** Mary Sandkamp, **Musashi Sakai;** Dan Thompson, **Yachiyo Chiba-ken/American Language Institute;** Carol Vaughn, **Kanto Kokusai High School. Osaka:** Lance Burrows, **Osaka Prefecture Settsu High School;** Bonnie Carpenter, **Mukogawa Joshi Daigaku/ Hannan Daigaku;** Josh Glaser, Richard Roy, **Human International University/Osaka Jogakuin Junior College;** Gregg Kennerly, **Osaka YMCA;** Ted Ostis, **Otemon University;** Chris Page, **ECC Language Institute;** Leon Pinsky, **Kwansei Gakuin University;** Chris Ruddenklau, **Kinki University;** John Smith, **Osaka International University. Saitama:** Marie Cosgrove, **Surugadai University. Kobe:** Donna Fujimoto, **Kobe University of Commerce. KOREA: Seoul:** Adrienne Edwards-Daugherty, Min Hee Kang, James Kirkmeyer, Paula Reynolds, Warren Weappa, Matthew Williams, **YBM ELS Shinchon;** Brian Cook, Jack Scott, Russell Tandy, **Hanseoung College. MEXICO: Mexico City:** Alberto Hern, **Instituto Anglo Americano de Idiomas;** Eugenia Carbonell, **Universidad Interamericana;** Cecilia Rey Gutiérrez, María del Rosario Escalada Ruiz, **Universidad Motolinia;** Raquel Márquez Colin, **Universidad St. John's;** Francisco Castillo, Carlos René Malacara Ramos, **CELE – UNAM/Mascarones;** Belem Saint Martin, **Preparatoria ISEC;** María Guadalupe Aguirre Hernández, **Comunidad Educativa Montessori;** Isel Vargas Ruelas, Patricia Contreras, **Centro Universitario Oparin;** Gabriela Juárez Hernández, Arturo Vergara Esteban Juan, **English Fast Center;** Jesús Armando Martínez Salgado, **Preparatoria Leon Tolstoi;** Regina Peña Martínez, **Centro Escolar Anahuac;** Guadalupe Buenrostro, **Colegio Partenon;** Rosendo Rivera Sánchez, **Colegio Anglo Español;** María Rosario Hernández Reyes, **Escuela Preparatoria Monte Albán;** Fernanda Cruzado, **Instituto Tecnológico del Sur;** Janet Harris M., **Colegio Anglo Español;** Rosalba Pérez Contreras, **Centro Lingüístico Empresarial. Ecatepec:** Diana Patricia Ordaz García, **Comunidad Educativa Montessori;** Leticia Ricart P., **Colegio Holandés;** Samuel Hernández B. **Instituto Cultural Renacimiento. Tlalpan:** Ana María Cortés, **Centro Educativo José P. Cacho. San Luis Potosi:** Sigi Orta Hernández, María de Guadalupe Barrientos J., **Instituto Hispano Inglés;** Antonieta Raya Z., **Instituto Potosino;** Gloria Carpizo, **Seminario Mayor Arquidiocesano de San Luis Potosí;** Susana Prieto Noyola, Silvia Yolanda Ortiz Romo **Universidad Politécnica de San Luis Potosí;** Rosa Arrendondo Flores, **Instituto Potosino/Universidad Champagnat;** María Cristina Carmillo, María Carmen García Leos, **Departamento Universitario de Inglés, UASLP;** María Gloria Candia Castro, **Universidad Tecnológica SLP;** Bertha Guadalupe Garza Treviño, **Centro de Idiomas, UASLP. Guadalajara:** Nancy Patricia Gómez Ley, **Escuela Técnica Palmares;** Gabriela Michel Vázquez, **Colegio Cervantes Costa Rica;** Abraham Barbosa Martínez, **Colegio Enrique de Osso;** Ana Cristina Plascencia Haro, Joaquín Limón Ramos, **Centro Educativo Tlaquepaque III;** Lucía Huerta Cervantes, Paulina Cervantes Fernández, Audrey Lizaola López, **Colegio Enrique de Osso,** Rocío de Miguel, **Colegio La Paz;** Jim Nixon, **Colegio Cervantes Costa Rica;** Hilda Delgado Parga, **Colegio D'Monaco;** Claudia Rodríguez, **English Key. León:** Laura Montes de la Serna, **Colegio Británico A.C.;** Antoinette Marie Hernández, **"The Place 4U2 Learn" Language School;** Delia Zavala Torres, Verónica Medellín Urbina, **EPCA Sur;** María Eugenia Gutiérrez Mena, Ana Paulina Suárez Cervantes, **Universidad la Salle;** Herlinda Rodríguez Hernández, **Instituto Mundo Verde,** María Rosario Torres Neri, **Instituto Jassa. Aguascalientes:** María Dolores Jiménez Chávez, **ECA – Universidad Autónoma de Aguascalientes;** María Aguirre Hernández, **ECA – Proyecto Start;** Fernando Xavier Goúrey O., **UAA – IEA "Keep On";** Felisia Guadalupe García Ruiz, **Universidad Tecnológica;** Margarita Zapiain B, Martha Ayala de la Concordia, Fernando Xavier Gomez Orenday, **Universidad Autónoma de Aguascalientes;** Gloria Aguirre Hernández, **Escuela de la Ciudad de Aguascalientes;** Hector Arturo Moreno Diaz, **Universidad Bonaterra.**

WorldView 3 Student Audio CD

(This CD contains all the material for Student Books 3A and 3B.)

TRACK	STUDENT BOOK PAGE	WORKBOOK PAGE	ACTIVITY	
1			Audio Program Introduction	
2	3	14	Unit 1	Listening
3	5	14	Unit 1	Pronunciation
4	7	17	Unit 2	Reading/Listening
5	8		Unit 2	Pronunciation
6	11	20	Unit 3	Listening
7	11	20	Unit 3	Pronunciation
8	11		Unit 3	Pronunciation
9	11	20	Unit 3	Pronunciation
10	15	23	Unit 4	Reading/Listening
11	16	23	Unit 4	Pronunciation
12	23	28	Unit 5	Listening
13	25	28	Unit 5	Pronunciation
14	25		Unit 5	Pronunciation
15	27		Unit 6	Pronunciation
16	27	31	Unit 6	Listening
17	31	34	Unit 7	Pronunciation
18	31	34	Unit 7	Pronunciation
19	31	34	Unit 7	Reading/Listening
20	35	37	Unit 8	Reading/Listening
21	37		Unit 8	Pronunciation
22	41	42	Unit 9	Listening
23	42	42	Unit 9	Pronunciation
24	45	45	Unit 10	Listening
25	47	45	Unit 10	Pronunciation
26	47	45	Unit 10	Pronunciation
27	49		Unit 11	Pronunciation
28	49	48	Unit 11	Listening
29	52	51	Unit 12	Pronunciation
30	53	51	Unit 12	Listening
31	61	56	Unit 13	Reading/Listening
32	63		Unit 13	Pronunciation
33	65	59	Unit 14	Listening
34	67	59	Unit 14	Pronunciation
35	68-69	62	Unit 15	Reading/Listening
36	70		Unit 15	Pronunciation
37	73	65	Unit 16	Listening
38	74	65	Unit 16	Pronunciation
39	79	70	Unit 17	Reading/Listening
40	81	70	Unit 17	Pronunciation
41	83	73	Unit 18	Listening
42	85		Unit 18	Pronunciation
43	87	76	Unit 19	Listening
44	87	76	Unit 19	Pronunciation
45	87	76	Unit 19	Pronunciation
46	91	79	Unit 20	Pronunciation
47	91	79	Unit 20	Listening
48	99	84	Unit 21	Reading/Listening
49	101	84	Unit 21	Pronunciation
50	103	87	Unit 22	Listening
51	105	87	Unit 22	Pronunciation
52	107	90	Unit 23	Listening
53	108	90	Unit 23	Pronunciation
54	110	93	Unit 24	Pronunciation
55	111	93	Unit 24	Reading/Listening
56	117		Unit 25	Pronunciation
57	117	98	Unit 25	Listening
58	121	101	Unit 26	Reading/Listening
59	122	101	Unit 26	Pronunciation
60	125	104	Unit 27	Listening
61	127	104	Unit 27	Pronunciation
62	129	107	Unit 28	Reading/Listening
63	130	107	Unit 28	Pronunciation
64		17	Unit 2	Extra Pronunciation Practice
65		28	Unit 5	Extra Pronunciation Practice
66		31	Unit 6	Extra Pronunciation Practice
67		37	Unit 8	Extra Pronunciation Practice
68		48	Unit 11	Extra Pronunciation Practice
69		48	Unit 11	Extra Pronunciation Practice
70		56	Unit 13	Extra Pronunciation Practice
71		62	Unit 15	Extra Pronunciation Practice
72		73	Unit 18	Extra Pronunciation Practice
73		98	Unit 25	Extra Pronunciation Practice